# The Historical Point of View in English Literary Criticism from 1570—1770

by

G. M. Miller

PHAETON PRESS
NEW YORK
1968

Originally Published 1913
Reprinted 1968





*Library of Congress Catalog Card Number 67-30906*

Published by Phaeton Press, Inc.

# Prefatory Note.

The completion of this study and its publication gives me the opportunity to pay my debt of thanks in this general way to various persons whose kindnesses have helped me during the period of its preparation. Besides this general acknowledgement I wish to thank specially Professor J. E. Spingarn and the authorities of the Clarendon Press for the chance to use the texts in Vol. III of the *Critical Essays of the Seventeenth Century* before the volume was issued from the press. I owe special thanks, also, to Professor Dr. Robert Petsch of the University of Liverpool for bibliographical suggestions; to Lektor Lionel R. M. Strachan of the University of Heidelberg for a painstaking reading of the text; and to Geh. Hofrat Hoops, editor of *Anglistische Forschungen*, for helpful criticisms and kindly encouragement during the preparation of the work. Finally I wish to make here special acknowledgement of my indebtedness to Professor Lewis E. Gates, whose teaching first introduced me to that historical study of English literary criticism out of which this present work has grown.

Cincinnati, December 21, 1911.

# Contents.

# I. Introduction.

## 1. Purpose and Incentive.

The purpose of this study is to trace the development of the historical point of view in English literary criticism from 1570 to 1770. In other words, the purpose of my investigation is to find out how far the historical point of view found expression in English literary criticism in the first two hundred years of its existence as a literary form.

The incentive for such a study comes from the fact that this particular phase of literary criticism, the early history of which I propose to investigate, has become of great importance in the last fifty years. Moreover, the history of literary criticism as a whole is itself a comparatively new field. The special works dealing with the general subject have all appeared within the last twenty years, and in general they have given but scant notice to my subject. Such earlier publications as Haslewood's *Ancient Critical Essays upon English Poets and Poesy* (1811—1815), various reprints by Arber, and the appearance from time to time of the critical essays of certain authors in connection with their complete works, furnished a certain amount of material, but had no adequate discussion of the history of literary criticism. The first utilization of this material as the basis for historical treatment occurred in 1891 in Schelling's *Poetic and Verse Criticism of the*

*Reign of Elizabeth*, an excellent little study, well illustrated by excerpts; but it covers only the field indicated by the title. In 1894 Laura Johnson Wylie published her *Studies in the Evolution of English Criticism*, a little work serving as a dissertation at Yale University, and, therefore, not particularly comprehensive. In 1896 Vaughan published his *English Literary Criticism*, a small volume of selections preceded by a good but brief historical introduction. The more significant books began with the publication in 1897 of Hamelius's *Kritik in der Englischen Literatur des 17. und 18. Jahrhunderts.* It is the first work to cover the whole period systematically from the Elizabethan critics to Wordsworth and Coleridge, and it covers it well, in spite of what appear to be a few errors in the classification of individual critics. Hamelius gives a chapter (pp. 161—182) to the "Begründung der historischen Kritik", but he says that it did not go back of Addison in origin and that it received its first expression in 1751. Gayley and Scott's *Methods and Materials of Literary Criticism* (1899) contains, for the few pages devoted to it (pp. 383—422), a surprisingly full and accurate outline of the development of literary criticism in England. The first edition of Spingarn's *History of Literary Criticism in the Renaissance* appeared in 1899. It broke new ground by applying the comparative method to the study of criticism, but, excellent as it is, since its aim is to cover the whole European field, it can spare but sixty pages to English criticism and it brings the study only down to Ben Jonson. Saintsbury's large three volume work (1900—1904), which he describes as *A History of Criticism and Literary Taste in Europe*, is a necessity to the student, but he deliberately ignores the historical point of view or notices it only to combat it, while his treatment of *Elizabethan Criticism* in the *Cambridge History of English Literature* (Vol. III, 1909) covers less than thirty pages. G. Gregory Smith's *Elizabethan Critical Essays* (1904) and Spingarn's *Critical Essays of the Seventeenth Century* (1908—1909), aim primarily to furnish complete collections of texts, but each has an excellent historical introduction. Smith denies the use of the historical point of view to any of the Elizabethan critics except to Daniel, while Spingarn points out very briefly its use by Bacon, Milton, Cowley, Sprat, Temple, Dennis, Dryden, Hume and Gibbon. On the whole, then, the aims and purposes even of those who have specially dealt with the history of English criticism have prevented any detailed investigation of the historical point of view, and the way remains clear for such a study.

## 2. Limits of the Investigation.

The limits of this investigation were announced in the first paragraph as the first two hundred years of English literary criticism, that is, from Ascham to Percy. There is considerable foundation for the conventional view that there were no complete formulations of the historical point of view as applied to literature before the middle of the eighteenth century. Indeed as late as 1800, the very year Wordsworth published his famous *Preface* to the second edition of the *Lyrical Ballads*, Madame de Staël-Holstein introduced her *De la Littérature Considérée dans ses Rapports avec les Institutions Sociales* with the words: "Je voulais montrer le rapport qui existe entre la littérature et les institutions sociales de chaque pays; et ce travail n'avait encore été fait dans aucun livre connu."[1] That nothing of the kind had appeared in "any known book" before 1800 was saying too much. Madame de Staël was not the original pioneer, as she should have known if she read the critics with any care, French, German and English; yet it is true that up to the beginning of the nineteenth century no one had deserved so much praise as de Staël for the boldness of her title and the comprehensiveness of her attempt.

It is unsafe, however, to assume that any distinct movement in human thought originated suddenly. At least thirty years before de Staël issued her *De la Littérature* there was a culmination in England of the transition from pseudo-classicism to romanticism. No small part of the change from Pope to Wordsworth took form in literary criticism, and one characteristic of much of this criticism was the expression in varying degrees of the historical point of view. But even this was not the beginning, and it is my special purpose to show in this study that, in the two hundred years before the transition in ideals reached such complete expression in the seventh decade of the eighteenth century, there were a number of tentative and even fairly bold expressions of the historical point of view. These expressions of the genetic conception of literature cannot be neglected in any adequate history of English literature, let alone in any history of criticism, because they acted as solvents of the dogmatic theories with which they were surrounded. They helped to prepare, in cumulative fashion, for the change in taste that finally resulted in the triumph of romanticism.

---

[1] *Œuvres Complètes*, I. 196.

That 1770 marks a natural division in the history of eighteenth century criticism can be shown by a brief enumeration of the chief critical works produced in the two decades preceding. In these twenty years there was not so much original literature produced; most of the novelists and the transition poets had begun their work before 1750. But from 1750 to 1770 such significant critical works appeared as Lowth's *Sacred Poetry of the Hebrews* (1753), Thomas Warton's *Observations on the Fairy Queen* (1754), Joseph Warton's *Essay on Pope* (Vol. I, 1756), *The Rambler* (1750–1752), *The Adventurer* (1753), *The Idler* (1758—1760), Hume's *Standard of Taste* (1757), Goldsmith's *Present State of Polite Learning* (1759), Young's *Conjectures on Original Composition* (1759), Hurd's *Letters on Chivalry and Romance* (1762), Macpherson's and Blair's *Dissertations* on *Ossian* (1762–1763), Brown's *History of the Rise and Progress of Poetry* (1764), Percy's *Essays* in his *Reliques* (1765), Johnson's *Preface* to his *Shakespeare* (1765), Wood's *Original Genius and Writings of Homer* (1768), and the letters on literary subjects of Gray, Walpole, Johnson, Shenstone and Percy.

It is not necessary for our purposes to do more than mention here works more purely on aesthetics, like Hogarth's *Analysis of Beauty* (1753), Burke's *Sublime and Beautiful* (1756), and Lord Kame's *Elements of Criticism* (1761). Neither is comment necessary on the significance for the general change in taste of such works as Macpherson's *Ossian* (1761), Walpole's *Castle of Otranto* (1764), and Percy's *Reliques* (1765). Only three or four critical works of any importance appeared after 1770 and before Wordsworth's *Prefaces* at the end of the century, and those were all written by men who had taken their critical position before 1770, and in three cases, at least, they had begun these later works before that date. Thomas Warton sent the first volume of his *History of English Poetry* to the printer in 1769, though the whole work did not appear until 1774—1781. Reynold's *Discourses* were published in 1778, but some of his material had already appeared in the *Idler* twenty years before. Joseph Warton's second volume of his *Essay on Pope* was published in 1782, but two hundred pages of it had been written and even printed twenty years before. In Johnson's *Lives of the Poets*, published in 1779—1781, his style is changed somewhat, but not his critical opinions. One may say, then, that by 1770 the critical work of the eighteenth century before Wordsworth and Coleridge had been practically completed.

This massing of significant critical works and the culmination in the general transition from pseudo-classicism to romanticism combine to make 1770 the natural *terminus ad quem* for an investigation into the earlier phases of the development of the historical point of view in English literary criticism. Moreover two noteworthy utterances by German contemporaries of the Wartons, Hurd and Wood help to confirm the choice of this date. In 1764 the genetic method was definitely applied to plastic art by Winckelmann in his *Geschichte der Kunst des Altertums*, and in 1767 Herder in *Fragmente über die neuere deutsche Litteratur* called as definitely for the extension of Winckelmann's method to literature. The titles of Winckelmann's headings alone will show his point of view: "Von den Ursachen der Verschiedenheit der Kunst unter den Völkern" — "Einfluß des Himmels in die Bildung" — "Einfluß des Himmels in die Denkungsart", etc.[1] He

[1] *Gesch. der Kunst*, pp. 28—34.

summarizes in a single sentence his belief — "Die Ursache und der Grund von dem Vorzuge, welchen die Kunst unter den Griechen erlangt hat, ist teils dem Einflusse des Himmels, teils der Verfassung und Regierung, und der dadurch gebildeten Denkungsart, wie nicht weniger der Achtung der Künstler und dem Gebrauche und der Anwendung zuzuschreiben."[1] Herder's cry for "ein Deutscher Winckelmann; der uns den Tempel der griechischen Weisheit und Dichtkunst so eröffne, als er den Künstlern das Geheimnis der Griechen von ferne gezeigt", is followed on the next page by a careful definition of the task to be accomplished.[2] Bernheim says Herder in the *Ideen zur Philosophie der Geschichte der Menschheit* (1784—1787) is the real founder of the modern conception of history;[3] but Herder had already laid the foundation for his later ideas here in the *Fragmente.* It is a commonplace now to point out the influence of English writers on Herder. Dr. Lambel, for instance, cites Blackwell as one of the strong influences on Herder's earlier work,[4] Hatch traces Shaftesbury's influence upon him,[5] and Kind shows how powerful an influence Young's *Conjectures* had upon him.[6] Though Herder and Winckelmann did not become immediately influential in English criticism, their work is of the highest significance as marking a definite stage in the European development of the historical point of view as applied to the arts, and this stage was reached in the decade between 1760 and 1770.

---

1 *Gesch. d. Kunst,* p. 96. Cf. Bosanquet's *History of Aesthetic,* p. 243.

2 *Fragmente,* Deutsche National-Lit., 76. Bd., 152.

3 *Lehrbuch der Historischen Methode,* p. 643.

4 *Einleitung* to *Fragmente,* ed. cited, xii.

5 *Stud. z. vergl. lit. Gesch.* I. 68—119.

6 *Edward Young in Germany,* pp. 40—57.

## 3. Possible Points of View in Literary Criticism.

It will be well before proceeding to discuss the critical material itself, to distinguish between the different possible points of view in literary criticism, to make clear what is meant by the historical point of view, and to see what outside helps may have come to the English critics.

In the formulation of the different possible points of view recent representative writers on literary criticism use different terminologies, but they have in mind largely the same things. J. A. Symonds in his essay *On Some Principles of Criticism* has a three-fold division of critical types, which he calls classical, romantic and scientific. "Classical criticism", he says, "rested upon a logical basis. It assumed the existence of certain fixed principles, from which correct judgments might be deduced. Romantic criticism substituted sympathies and antipathies for rules, and exchanged authority for personal opinion. Scientific criticism proceeds by inductions, historical investigation, morphological analysis, misdoubting the certainty of aesthetic principles, regarding the instincts and sensibilities of the individual with distrust, seeking the material for basing the canons of perfection upon some positive foundation."[1]

Saintsbury, in his essay on *The Kinds of Criticism* does not formulate his categories so clearly, but a reader can gather that the three types he has in mind are the judicial, the personal and the scientific. By judicial he would mean judging not on the basis of rules for fixed abstract "kinds", nor on the basis of aesthetic or philosophical principles and not on the basis of moral or extra-

[1] *Essays, Speculative and Suggestive,* p. 60.

literary canons of any kind, but on the basis of a comparative method. He is opposed to any personal or impressionistic method and even more opposed to what he says is the impossible scientific method.[1] In the opening chapter of his *History of Criticism* he defines criticism as, "that function of the judgment which busies itself with the goodness or badness, the success or ill-success, of literature from the purely literary point of view", and "the reasoned exercise of literary taste" (I. 1 and 2), and throughout the book there are incidental references to the types he does not believe in or does not like.

Gates in his essay on *Impressionism and Appreciation* insists that a sound appreciative method in criticism, which he believes to be the most desirable type, must be based on a combination of what he would call the historical, psychological, impressionistic, comparative and aesthetic points of view.[2]

Wernaer in his article on *The New Constructive Criticism* summarizes his thought by saying that the true critic must combine the different types, impressionistic, aesthetic, appreciative and judicial, but he seems to misunderstand Gates's use of "appreciation", and his new judicial criticism is to be based on all the others and include a knowledge of historical conditions.[3]

Hoskins in discussing *Biological Analogy in Literary Criticism* asserts that only some sort of evolutionary theory in psychological form can bring order out of the chaos arising from the conflicting points of view assumed by

---

[1] Cf. Introductory Essay in *Essays in English Literature.*

[2] Cf. in *Studies and Appreciations* the essay cited (pp. 205—234) and the one on Taine.

[3] *Pubs. Mod. Lang. Assoc.* XXII. 445.

the aesthetic, biographical and historical methods of literary study.[1]

Spingarn in his *Introduction* to his *Critical Essays of the Seventeenth Century*, when he points out the different possibilities, says of that century: "Nearly all the moods of criticisms, classical and romantic, analytical and synthetic, impressionistic and dogmatic, historical and interpretative, are fitfully represented there" (I. p. cvi). In a booklet on *The New Criticism* just published (1911), Spingarn apparently uses the terms "appreciative" and "impressionistic" interchangeably, while he contrasts with this point of view the various "objective" and "dogmatic" forms of criticism, mentioning as subdivisions the "historical", the "psychological", the "dogmatic", and the "aesthetic" (p. 3—9). In the sketch of the development of criticism that follows this classification he says, "Very early in the century [the nineteenth], Mme. de Staël and others formulated the idea that Literature is an 'expression of society'" (p. 11.) — a statement that might imply the absence of such formulation before 1800.[2]

Such are the categories used in a few representative discussions of the different points of view in criticism from 1893 to 1911. But to avoid the confusion arising from the use of different names for the same thing I shall

---

[1] *Mod. Phil.* VII. 20. Cf. Hoskin's article on *The Place and Function of a Standard in a Genetic Theory of Literary Development, Pubs. Mod. Lang. Assoc.* XXV. 379—402.

[2] D. Nichol Smith's suggestive lecture on *The Function of Criticism* (Oxford, 1909) reached me too late to summarize it in the discussion above. The "three definite points, on one of which, or all of which, criticism must base itself" are "the date, the author, and the work" (p. 15); by which Smith means (1) the historical point of view, (2) the biographical point of view, and (3) various phases of dogmatic, aesthetic, impressionistic and appreciative criticism.

attempt to formulate these different points of view in a more systematic fashion.

In the first place an analysis of the points of view in criticism makes it evident that the widest possible division is on the basis of relation to the critic himself into objective, subjective and a combination of these two, which we may call subjective-objective. Of the first head we may make a two-fold division — judicial and scientific and each of these can be still further divided. The judicial critic judges, ranks, classifies, by some sort of fixed standards. The standards themselves are consciously formulated, either on the basis of tradition or on the basis of aesthetic or other general principles. If they are formulated from tradition, the critic takes the dogmatic point of view. He believes in abstractions called "Epic", "Tragedy", and so on. Any specimen of these different literary kinds he tries and judges in accordance with rules which are the formulation of the ideals for each type by great critics — Aristotle, Horace and the French critics — in accordance with the practice of great writers — Homer, Aeschylus, Virgil — who wrote models of the type. Such dogmatic criticism considers a literary work objectively with little reference to its relations to the author, that is, to the psychology of its creation — or its relation to the reader, that is, its psychological effect. The rules are intended to serve two purposes, to make the resulting work both delight and teach. Hence the dogmatic point of view, in addition to certain artistic formulas, introduces an extra-literary standard in the form of a conscious moral test. Such criticism as this found constant expression in England for nearly three centuries, and perhaps has not altogether disappeared yet.

When the critic judges by aesthetic standards, he draws these standards from the experience of readers in contact with works of literary art. A psychological analysis of the mental states resulting from such contact makes possible the formulation of the general principles and elements of beauty, which constitute the appeal of art, and on the basis of these principles the aesthetic critic judges. Naturally there was little attempt at the formulation of such aesthetic principles in the formative sixteenth century or in the seventeenth, when, in general, the "rules" held sway; but since the beginning of the eighteenth century aesthetic principles have been more and more discussed.

The scientific or genetic point of view, considers a literary work in relation to the forces controlling its origin and production. It is a specimen to be explained. It is an effect, the causes of which may be analyzed and formulated under two heads. The first of these heads is the personal psychology of the author and its causal relation to the work in question. This psychological or biographical point of view considers the contribution of the author's individuality, his personality, his peculiar temperament to his work. It seeks to trace the individual qualities of any particular piece of literary work back to their sources in the individual qualities of the author. But a further investigation would not consider many of these personal qualities as final sources. And so the scientific point of view may also formulate its explanation of a literary work in terms of its historical environment, in terms of the general forces controlling its origin and production, by their influence upon its author. The recognition of these forces — racial, national, epochal —

of the matrix of ideas, political, religious, moral, social, economic, philosophical, scientific, artistic, literary, out of which a literary work is born — this constitutes the historical point of view in literary criticism.[1]

The point of view wholly subjective is generally named impressionistic, though, as we have seen, it has been called also romantic and personal. Criticism in this case is written wholly from the standpoint of the personal impression made upon the critic. Such criticism is wholly individual. The ideal impressionistic critic becomes a delicate sensitive instrument upon which each individual work of art records its individual quality, and it is the business of the impressionist critic to reproduce for the benefit of others the peculiar shiver he has for each poem, each line, each word. His criticism is sensuous rather than intellectual. The name Symonds has given to this type, "romantic criticism", is suggestive of its origin and history, because it is only since the triumph of romanticism that it has become a clearly marked critical type.

When the critic combines the objective and the subjective points of view, probably the best name for the result is appreciative criticism. This combination is the highest phase of literary criticism as an art. Symonds says: "The true critic must combine all three types [classical, romantic and scientific] in himself, and hold the balance by his sense of their reciprocal relations."[2] All the writers I have quoted have insisted on a combination of points of view, and Gates with especial felicity and effectiveness.[3] Even Saintsbury, in spite of his antipathy

---

[1] Cf. the definition of Hamelius, work cited, p. 166.

[2] Work cited, p. 62.

[3] Work cited, pp. 218 and 233.

for the words "aesthetic," "scientific" and "personal," practically calls for a combination of the points of view I have been trying to define.[1] The appreciative point of view involves, then, first, the native endowment of the impressionist — a delicate sensitiveness to the peculiar charm of each separate piece of literature. But the appreciative critic must not stop short with the impressionist's feeling and the reproduction of that feeling; he must make clear *why* he feels so and so.

The equipment of the appreciative critic must include, therefore, a thorough acquaintance with literature itself, as it has manifested itself in different periods and in different authors and even in different countries. Such an equipment will afford the necessary material for the comparative method, the best phase of dogmatic criticism. Then he must have an adequate understanding of aesthetic principles. Aesthetic principles and the comparative method just mentioned will provide him with objective standards. In addition to these he must have an understanding of the personal psychology of the author and its relation to his work. And finally he must have a thorough knowledge of the historical environment of the author and of his work. All these, however, are merely means to an end — an apprehension of the unique appeal of each piece of literature and a comprehension of the various forces that have combined to make this unique appeal, so that the appeal itself may be brought home to the reader of the criticism. If the appreciative critic is to accomplish his task he must combine the best in the critical methods of Anatole France, Matthew Arnold, Walter Pater, Sainte-Beuve and Taine.

---

[1] Cf. *Essays in English Literature,* p. xvi.

## 4. The Historical Point of View.

It must be premised, then, that it is unsafe to make extravagant claims for the historical method in literary criticism, and there must be due recognition that the method is open to abuse. In his famous criticism of Taine, Sainte-Beuve points out what the abuse of the historical method may result in, when he says that the proper title of the *History of English Literature* should be, "Histoire de la race et de la civilisation anglaises par la littérature."[1] Yet Sainte-Beuve recognizes fully the force of the three influences Taine formulated; his objection is that Taine's formula does not provide for the analysis of individual genius,[2] the work he himself had done so well.[3] The great value of the genetic method in literary history proper is now generally recognized,[4] but for literary criticism it must not be forgotten that it is only a means, though an indispensable means, to an end — a finer and truer appreciative criticism.

The historical point of view as applied to literature, in the form known to us since the latter part of the eighteenth century, is the result chiefly of two forces — that interest in the past which makes up a large part of the romantic revolt against early eighteenth century liter-

---

[1] *Nouveaux Lundis*, VIII. 67. Cf. Scherer, *Essays on Eng. Lit.*, p. 74.

[2] Work cited, pp. 68—69. Cf. Dutoit, *Die Theorie des Milieu*, p. 80.

[3] Cf. Brandes, *Die Hauptströmungen der Literatur des 19. Jahrhunderts*, V. 285.

[4] Cf. Ten Brink, *Über die Aufgabe der Literaturgeschichte*, pp. 51—52; Dilthey, *Die Einbildungskraft des Dichters*, pp. 471 and 474; Falkenheim, *Kuno Fischer und die Literarhistorische Methode*, pp. 24—25; Smith, *The Functions of Criticism*, pp. 4—9.

ary ideals,[1] and the growth of science and its application in the form of genetic history to the various phases of man's social life and artistic activities. Because these forces did not come into full play until the latter part of the eighteenth century and the first part of the nineteenth, there were no complete formulations or applications of the historical point of view as a method of approach to literature or art before the middle of the eighteenth century.[2]

Philosophically the historical point of view in literary criticism rests upon the general principles of the organic unity of national or community life and its historical continuity.[3] The first of these principles makes up one phase of that genetic conception of history, which considers, in the language of Bernheim, "daß die verschiedenen Betätigungen der Menschen in innerlichem Zusammenhang und in Wechselwirkung miteinander und mit den physischen Bedingungen stehen."[4] As factors in this organic unity, we must consider, then, not merely inherited racial characteristics, but also the total national environment—physical surroundings, government, social institutions and relations, religion, philosophy, science and art and their causal relations one with the other. The conception of historical continuity is also genetic, since it involves the conception of causal connection between successive ages.[5] This historical attitude is the direct result of the modern scientific spirit, of the desire to understand, to comprehend,

---

[1] Cf. Beers, *History of English Romanticism in the Eighteenth Century,* pp. 2 and 24, and Phelps, *The Beginnings of the English Romantic Movement,* Chs. VI, VII and VIII.

[2] Cf. above, p. 4.

[3] Cf. Gates, work cited, p. 197.

[4] Work cited, p. 29.

[5] Cf. Bernheim's definition of history, work cited, p. 8.

to explain the past by cause and effect.[1] The historical spirit, then, when applied in literary study or criticism, calls for a consideration of causes, of origins, and of development as related to causes.

The necessity for the application of this method in literary study has been recognized by leading critics from the middle of the eighteenth century. Even such men as Dr. Johnson and Jeffrey have recognized its necessity. In 1765 Johnson said, "Every man's performance, to be rightly estimated, must be compared with the state of the age in which he lived, and with his own particular opportunities."[2] As Gates points out, Jeffrey used it in his reviews of Ford's *Dramatic Works* (1811), de Staël's *De la Littérature* (1812) and of *Wilhelm Meister's Apprenticeship* (1825).[3] Carlyle in 1831 in his review of Taylor's *Historic Survey of German Poetry* said that "the History of a nation's Poetry is the essence of its History, political, economic, scientific, religious," and he asserts that the complete historian of poetry "will discern the grand spiritual Tendency of each period, what was the highest Aim and Enthusiasm of mankind in each, . . . . for by this the Poetry of the nation modulates itself; this *is* the Poetry of the nation."[4] Pater says in his essay on *Winckelmann* that "individual genius works ever under conditions of time and place," and, "criticism must never forget that 'the artist is the child of his time.'"[5] Gates sums the

---

[1] Cf. Bernheim, pp. 184 ff.

[2] *Eighteenth Century Essays on Shakespeare*, p. 132.

[3] *Selections from the Essays of Francis Jeffrey*, p. xxvii; cf. also the essay on Ford, pp. 1—20.

[4] *Critical and Miscellaneous Essays*, II. 341—342. Cf. Roe, *Carlyle as a Critic of Literature*, pp. 51—54.

[5] *The Renaissance*, pp. 209—210.

matter up, when he says that the appreciative critic "believes that the generating pleasures that produced the work of art, and that once thrilled in a single human spirit, in response to the play and counterplay upon him, of the life of his time, must remain permanently the central core of the energy in the work; and that only as he comes to know those pleasures with fine intimacy, can he conjure out of the work of art its perfect acclaim of delight for now and here."[1]

One particular result of the historical point of view, honestly and persistently assumed in literary criticism, is historical tolerance. Its assumption tends to dissolve prejudice, because it brings knowledge. It tries to look at a work of art not merely from the point of view of the critic's own age or nation, but with the eyes of the artist's own contemporaries and fellow countrymen. It is the answer to Spingarn's question in his review of Saintsbury's *History of Criticism* — "How did the modern conception of a relative aesthetic, varying from age to age, from country to country, arise in a period, which, according to Mr. Saintsbury, was one simply of 'eighteenth century orthodoxy'?"[2] The study of the development of the historical point of view in literary criticism means, therefore, the study of the development of such a relative aesthetic, with all that may imply in the destruction of dogmatic standards, and in the increased capacity of the critic, through the increase of his historical tolerance and sympathies, to enjoy and make others enjoy the work of widely differing men, periods and even nations.

---

[1] *Studies and Appreciations*, p. 218; but cf. the whole essay on *Impressionism and Appreciation*, especially pp. 216—19.

[2] *Mod. Phil.* I. 482.

## 5. The Background of Foreign Critical Utterances.

It has already been pointed out that at the close of the period we are considering Winckelmann and Herder gave pronouncements on the historical point of view of the highest importance. Their work marked a definite stage in the development of the genetic conception of the arts. Though they came too late to influence the Englishmen writing at the end of this period, they themselves, and especially Herder, were affected by the work of English critics and philosophers. Earlier expressions of the historical point of view, however, are not wanting in Italian, French and even Spanish, both in criticism and in the general theory and practice of history itself, and many of these expressions did influence English criticism directly or indirectly. It is important, therefore, to know something of this foreign background of the first two hundred years of English criticism.

The foreign critics of Renaissance times who seemed to have some conception of the historical standpoint were comparatively less important to English criticism than their more dogmatic brethren. Spingarn points out a number of continental critics between 1554 and 1628 who gave expression, more or less tentatively, to the historical point of view. His enumeration includes Giraldi Cintio, Pigna, Patrizzi, la Cueva, Lope de Vega, Sanchez and Ogier.[1] These men may not have been especially influential on English criticism, but men like Giraldi Cintio and Lope de Vega were at least known to Renaissance Englishmen.[2]

[1] *Lit. Crit. in Ren.*, pp. 112, 116, 162, 165—166, 233—236.

[2] Daniel's certain acquaintance with Cintio is proved by an unmistakable reference. Cf. Gregory Smith, II. 360 and note.

There is no doubt, however, about the influence upon English criticism of the French critics of the later seventeenth and earlier eighteenth centuries. The assertion of such an influence is a commonplace of English literary history. Among these French critics were men who gave expression to views out of harmony with the conventional dogmatism of their times, men who expressed doubts of the universal validity of the rules and of reason as all-sufficient guides in the arts, who saw something of the necessity of considering the social and historical forces enveloping a literary work, if they were to arrive at a just estimate of its worth.

The best known of these French literary rebels to Englishmen was Saint-Évremond. Owing to his long residence in England and his extraordinarily wide acquaintance in the social and literary life of London, his ideas were known through personal contact, as well as through his essays, to all contemporary English critics and men of letters.[1] The English translations of his essays in 1685 and 1686 Spingarn thinks "were probably the first volumes of critical essays that ever appeared in England."[2] His essays, *Concerning Ancient and Modern Tragedy*, *On the Tragedies*, *On our Comedies*, *Concerning English Comedy*, *Observations on the Taste and Discernment of the French*, *On the Poems of the Ancients*, and *Concerning the Marvellous*, were all grist for the English critical mill. His attacks on the rules and authority and his exaltation of genius,[3] his assertion and re-assertion that difference in natural surroundings, religion, government, customs,

[1] Cf. Daniels, *Saint-Évremond en Angleterre, passim.*

[2] Spingarn, *Crit. Essays,* III. 308.

[3] *Œuvres,* III. 280—281.

manners and taste must mean a difference in literature, that if Homer were writing today he would write admirable poems, but they would be adapted to the century in which he was writing (IV. 325–337) — all this was of great importance in England at a time when pseudo-classicism was rampant.

Fontenelle was also important, with his discussion of differences in "times, governments, and affairs in general." He delights in his paradox "that if our trees are as great as those of former times, we can equal Homer, Plato and Demosthenes." He suggests that the soil of France may be no better adapted to the reasonings of the Egyptians than to their palms. He states positively that eloquence and poetry depend principally upon the vivacity of the imagination, and the imagination "does not need a long series of experiences or a great quantity of rules to have all the perfection of which it is capable."[1] Such a statement must have made the dogmatists hold up their hands in horror. The *Digressions sur les Anciens et les Modernes*, in which these attacks on the rules and the assertion of the necessary relativity of literary standards because of diversity of environment are found, appeared in 1688.

It is worth noting that the two men just discussed cannot be claimed as fighting wholly for the Moderns in the quarrel then raging, and both respected the Ancients. The next Frenchman of importance to us, may be counted, on the whole, as a defender, though a very reasonable defender, of the Ancients. The *Réflexions Critiques sur*

---

[1] *Œuvres Diverses*, VI. 207, 210, 215, 221. Note that Saintsbury says of this part of the *Digressions*, "Here he becomes scientific, and therefore necessarily ceases to be of importance in literature". *Hist. of Crit.*, II. 506. Cf. his treatment of de Staël, III. 101—102.

*la Poesie et sur la Peinture* of Abbé Du Bos did not appear until 1719, but it went through seven editions before 1770, and was translated into English in 1748. Lombard says that slowly and confusedly a new aesthetic emerged from the Quarrel of the Ancients and the Moderns, and that in reality the development of the modern historical and comparative point of view can be traced directly back to the Quarrel and to the defenders of the Ancients.[1] The same writer points out that Du Bos attempted to give a scientific answer to the question that had proved so embarrassing to the defenders of the Ancients, the question as to whether humanity is progressing or not, by showing that neither Perrault nor Madame Dacier was right, but that the course of humanity rises and falls, re-arises and re-falls. Du Bos expressed this idea as early as 1695 in a letter to Bayle. Between that date and 1619 he deserted Cartesianism and became a follower of Locke and the English philosophy. To explain the rise and fall of humanity he worked out his theory of climate, expressed it first in 1705, again in 1709, and finally with great fullness in 1719 in the *Réflexions Critiques*.[2]

Du Bos says in the *Avertissement*, "I am looking for the cause which is able to make some periods so productive and others so sterile in celebrated artists."[3] Almost all of the second volume is given up to this search for causes. The first few sections in the volume try to answer the question, "What is genius?" and the first sentence summarizes the whole discussion — "The sublime of poesie and of painting is to touch and to please" (I. 1). This

---

[1] *La Querelle des Anciens et des Modernes; l'Abbé Du Bos*, p. 23.

[2] Lombard, work cited, p. 36 ff.

[3] *Réflexions* I. i.

definition builds the foundation for his doctrine that it is no longer necessary to obey authorities, whether Aristotle or Bossu; for if the one test of genius is the appeal to the feelings, then sentiment, and not reason, is the sole judge and neither reason nor authority have any rights in the case (II. 538). This is, of course, only the doctrine of taste, the "je ne sais quoi," of those who, willingly or unwillingly, found a grace beyond the rules.[1] Du Bos later turns the doctrine of sentiment with great success in favor of the Ancients.[2]

Du Bos gives up two hundred pages, however, to his main task, an exposition of the causes why genius appears at certain times and in certain countries and at other times does not. A summary is unfair to him, for his exposition is made clear by a wealth of illustration, but briefly he finds the controlling influences on the development of genius are both moral and physical. Genius depends originally upon the happy constitution of the brain; but the brain is strongly influenced by qualities of the air and natural environment, influences more or less stimulating or soothing. These natural influences direct the development of the national spirit or genius and so also help to control the moral influences, government, religion, and so on, exercised upon individual genius, and retarding or encouraging its development (II. 320 ff.).

One can hardly say that Saint-Évremond or Fontenelle got anything from their English contemporaries, but Du Bos was directly influenced by Locke, Wotton and Addison. He himself was quoted by later English critics, like Brown and the Wartons. We can probably say safely, with

---

[1] Cf. Spingarn, *Crit. Essays,* I. c.

[2] Cf. the last sections of Vol. II.

Lombard[1], that Du Bos influenced all contemporary and succeeding critics, whether they cite him or not; the unusual number of editions of his *Réflexions* would alone show his importance.

## 6. Historical Theory and Practice.

It is proper here to mention the writers who may have helped toward the development of the historical view in criticism by works, either in theory or in practice, contributing to the growth of the genetic conception of history proper. Only one work before the eighteenth century is discussed at any length by the authorities.[2] Jean Bodin's *Methodus ad facilem historiarum cognitionem* appeared in 1566, and his *De republica* in 1576. Flint says that Bodin aimed at a real explanation of events through two classes of influences, climate and political causes, but that in stating the influence of climate he had been preceded by Hippocrates, Plato, Aristotle, Polybius and Galen.[3] Bodin probably had little if any direct influence on English criticism, though he is mentioned by Sidney[4] and Harvey[5] and twice by Bolton.[6]

---

[1] Work cited, p. 44.

[2] Cf. for bibliographical references on various sixteenth century treatises on the writing of history, Spingarn, *Critical Essays of the Seventeenth Century*, I. 238—239. Cf. further for the influence of the Italians on English historical writers, Einstein, *The Italian Renaissance in England*, pp. 308—313.

[3] *History of the Philosophy of History*, p. 197. Cf. Bernheim, *Lehrbuch der Historischen Methode*, p. 194ff.

[4] Letter to his brother Robert, Collins' reprint of Arber's *Critical Essays and Literary Fragments*, p. 6.

[5] Smith, *Eliz. Crit. Essays*, II. 281.

[6] Spingarn, *Critical Essays*, I. 87, 93.

Vico did his first work practically at the same time as Du Bos. Bernheim names him, along with Bodin, as one of the two real prophets of the new genetic conception of history.[1] Flint points out the strong influence of Bacon on Vico.[2] Vico first gave utterance to his views in a university lecture in 1719. In 1720 and 1721 appeared his essays on the unity and constancy of jurisprudence, and in supplementary notes to these in 1722 he first expressed his anticipation of the Wolfian and other later views on Homer. In 1725 the first edition of his *Principles of a New Science* appeared, in which he tries to get at "the common nature of nations, in which all knowledge, science, art, religion, morality, political and juridical systems, are originated and developed."[3] In the second edition of the *New Science* in 1730, he gave a whole book to the development of his theories about Homer. Flint declares that Vico anticipated every general position maintained by Wolf, and Hermann's and Lachmann's hypotheses as well.[4]

Though Vico seems to have had no immediate influence in England, certain Frenchmen, contemporaries of his, did have such an influence. Lenglet du Fresnoy's *Methode pour étudier l'histoire* was published in 1713. Montesquieu's *Considérations sur les causes de la grandeur des Romains et de leur décadence* in 1734 was "the first work in which a sustained and comprehensive attempt was made to show how the events and course of history have been determined by general physical and moral

[1] Bernheim, work cited, p. 641.

[2] *Vico,* 31, 33.

[3] Flint, *Vico,* p. 35.

[4] *Vico*, 176.

causes".[1] His famous *L'esprit des lois* in 1748 was, of course, known everywhere; but the five books of this work on the connection between the laws and other results of man's social life and such natural forces as temperature, soil and food, Flint says had been fully anticipated by Bodin[2], and Du Bos had applied the same methods to the study of literature nearly thirty years before. After Montesquieu's works came Turgot's *Discours sur les progrès successifs de l'esprit humain* in 1750, and in 1756 Voltaire's *Essai sur l'histoire generale et sur les moeurs et l'esprit des Nations depuis Charlemagne jusqu'a nos jours.* In 1765 Voltaire first used the phrase "*La Philosophie de l'Histoire*", though he did not use it in our sense and our modern idea was first expounded completely by Herder in 1784. Nevertheless Montesquieu, Turgot and Voltaire gave great impetus to the philosophical study of history. Their influence was felt at once in England, while two of them, at least, Montesquieu and Voltaire, had themselves been influenced by the English.

The background of historical theory in English itself is comparatively slight. Such men as Bacon, Bolton, Hume and Gibbon, because of their more intimate connection with criticism, will be noticed in their proper places in the chapters to follow. Only one man of any renown need be considered here, and that is Lord Bolingbroke. His *Letters on the Study and Use of History* were not published until 1752, but they were privately printed before his death in 1751 and the first one is dated 1735. They were written during his exile in France and only one year later than Montesquieu's book on the grandeur

---

[1] Flint, *Hist. of the Philos. of Hist.,* p. 263.

[2] *Ibid.,* p. 198.

and the decadence of the Romans; but they preceded in composition the much more significant work in historical theory just discussed, the three books of Montesquieu, Turgot and Voltaire.

The true purpose of the study of history, Bolingbroke says in the first *Letter*, is neither to furnish mere personal amusement, a fault common in England, nor to acquire material for conversational and rhetorical display, a common fault in France. Neither is the purpose of such study merely to find out what is historical fact. He has little patience with those scholars who are content to do no more than collect, compile and sift historical material.[1] History is rather to be of positive and practical use to man. Its "true and proper object . . . is a constant improvement in private and in public virtue"—it is "philosophy teaching by examples" (p. 1). History is a necessity to those who have to do with government, to the statesman and the citizen, because the experience of the past teaches them to judge the present and the future. Moreover, history has a profound ethical and cultural value for the individual, because it "serves to purge the mind of those national partialities and prejudices"—"that ridiculous and hurtful vanity by which the people of each country are apt to prefer themselves to those of every other, and to make their own customs and manners and opinions the standards of right and wrong, of true and false" (p. 9—10) —an excellent statement on historical tolerance.

These are the ends of the study of history, as Bolingbroke conceives them, a conception in harmony with the growing spirit of his age, that nothing can justify its existence which is not useful to man, and really no more

[1] *Letters on the Study and Use of History,* pp. 1—3.

than a re-phrasing and application to history of the Horatian maxim of the ends of poetry—to delight and to teach. To secure these ends, history must be composed in accordance with right methods. It must appeal not only to the imagination but also to the reason and the judgment. He summarizes his ideal of method for "authentic histories" in a single sentence—"we shall find many a complete series of events, preceded by a deduction of their immediate and remote causes, related in their full extent, and accompanied with such a detail of circumstances and characters, as may transport the attentive reader back to the very time, make him a party to the councils, and an actor in the whole scene of affairs" (p. 36).

It would be hard to overestimate the relative importance of such an ideal for historical method—a combination of picturesque compelling narrative with a philosophical analysis of causes—when given forth by a man who bulked so large in the eyes of his time as Bolingbroke. It was a sign—both effect and cause—of one of the most important intellectual movements in the eighteenth century—the awakening interest in history. Its absolute value is probably much less.[1] Bolingbroke sneers at investigators into original sources—the same class of men as those who in our own day think themselves alone entitled to be called historians. He allows some virtue to the harmless drudges "who make fair copies of foul manuscripts", because they "enable others to study with greater ease"; but as for men "of the first rank in learning, and to whom the whole tribe of scholars bow with reverence", men like Scaliger

[1] Cf. Stephen, *History of English Thought in the Eighteenth Century*, II. 173—175; Grant, *English Historians*, pp. xxvii—xxxi.

and Usher, he avows "a thorough contempt for the whole business of these learned lives". His quarrel with them is two-fold, first, that they bend their facts to fit a system imposed from without, and, second, that they fail to serve the true ends of history. As for himself he would rather commit any number of blunders in chronology, "than sacrifice half my life to collect all the learned lumber that fills the head of an antiquary". Moreover, he has the naive idea that these scholarly investigators have already collected all the possible materials of history, and all that is needed now is the correct writing up of this material.[1] It is true, also, that his conception of historical causation is limited in scope. It does not rise to the plane of Montesquieu's *Spirit of the Laws.* Indeed, like other English leaders in eighteenth century thought, Hume and Adam Smith[2], for example, Bolingbroke in general, refused to consider the influence of environment, especially physical environment, upon historical development. The only work on historical methods he mentions specially is "the method of Bodin, a man famous in his time"; yet he mentions it only to condemn it, especially "a tedious fifth chapter, wherein he accounts for the characters of nations according to their positions on the globe".[3] He saw with great clearness the part played in history by the motives, the passions, the personal interests and ambitions of princes, ministers, and party leaders; conscious intrigue, diplomacy, as historical forces, would appeal most to a practical politician like Bolingbroke or to the school of thinkers and moralists to which he and his leading contemporaries belonged, men who believed that the principles of common human nature, a contagion of manners and a clash of individual human wills ought to be sufficient to account for everything human.[1]

Yet Leslie Stephen goes too far when he asserts that Bolingbroke "characteristically begins by depriving himself of the necessary materials for researches", that he "manages with curious infelicity to repudiate the true historical method before it has come into being", and that he failed to have "any clear conception of the unity and continuity of history".[2] Judged in the light of our modern conception of historical methods and purposes Bolingbroke's achievement is not so great, but relatively and historically it is decidedly important. He insists on a critical examination of authorities and sources (p. 29—32). He sees the special value of a study of modern history (pp. 49—51), and recommends the study of the "materia historica" for such modern history—memorials, collections of public acts and monuments, of private letters, and of treaties, and even oral tradition. His statement of causes and his understanding of the connection between events is not wholly superficial, a matter of "the back stairs theory of politics", as Stephen asserts.[3] In his sketch of European history from 1659 to 1688 *(Letter VII.)* Bolingbroke accounts for the success of France by a careful analysis of the personalities of Louis XIV and his great ministers, and by a definite citation of the influence of "the soil, the climate, the situation of France, the ingenuity, the

---

[1] Cf. Patten, work cited, p. 227 ff.

[2] Work cited, II. 173—175.

[3] Work cited, II. 174.

industry, the vivacity of her inhabitants" (p. 69). He marked out the paths which eighteenth century history was to take.[1] Few men of his time influenced more men in more directions. He was the mentor of Pope. Burke and the Pitts, father and son, got something of their eloquence and part of their political inspiration from him. Voltaire was glad to acknowledge his indebtedness to his great English friend. Hume and Gibbon show his influence not only in style and tone and ideas but also in actual historical method.

Bolingbroke himself regrets the little accomplished in the actual writing of history in England as compared with what had been accomplished on the continent (p. 57). Yet a number of influences since the beginning of the sixteenth century had been making for the development of historical writing of a higher class. The Renaissance divorced philosophy from theology. Bishop Creighton declares that the growth of national feeling is the most distinctive mark separating historically the modern world from the medieval.[2] The Reformation meant the assertion of nationality against the medieval conception of a European commonwealth. National consciousness and pride in national achievement in Elizabethan times found expression chiefly in historical chronicles in both prose and poetry and in the great historical drama. The character of the struggle between King and Parliament in the Civil war was a direct incentive to the study of the national past as a practical means of proving political contentions. The questions of the Revolution of 1688 still further emphasized the necessity for historical study. The dis-

[1] Cf. Grant, work cited, p. 28.

[2] Introductory note to the *Cambridge Modern History*, I. 2.

cussion of the principles of government entered the domain of philosophy in the work of Hobbes and Locke, and the movement they represented was bound to call out a careful investigation of the past. The prevailing rationalistic philosophy at the end of the seventeenth and the beginning of the eighteenth century tended to encourage the study of cause and effect in the sequence of events. The skeptical and deistic movements in the early eighteenth century contributed both negatively and positively to historical conceptions.[1] The rise of science through the influence of such men as Bacon and the founders of the Royal Society lent its aid to the inductive study of all kinds of facts and to the conception of the continuity of natural law. Even the movement toward plainness, simplicity and truth in literary style at the end of the seventeenth and beginning of the eighteenth century had a helpful reaction on the tone and spirit of historical writing. By the middle of the eighteenth century the cumulative effect of all these forces had prepared the way for the great triumvirate, Hume, Robertson and Gibbon.[2]

In the meantime the actual collection of historical materials and the writing of history increased with the demand. The masses of the collections began in the age of Elizabeth. The Cotton and the Bodleian libraries were founded then. Selden and other antiquaries continued in the seventeenth and eighteenth centuries the work begun by Camden in the sixteenth century. Multiplying collec-

---

[1] Cf. Stephen, work cited, I. 166—168, 191—193, 263—271 (Middleton).

[2] Cf. Flint's *History of the Philosophy of History,* pp. 28—42, for a discussion of the forces influential on the growth of historical theory and practice.

tions of various kinds finally resulted in the foundation of the British Museum in 1753. Historical writing itself increased rather slowly in the seventeenth century. The contemporary and autobiographical nature of a good deal of the seventeenth century history is well illustrated in its two best known works, Lord Clarendon's *History of the Great Rebellion,* and Bishop Burnet's *History of My Own Times.* Both these works illustrate another interesting fact — the great increase in the publication of historical works beginning with 1700. The first part of Clarendon's history was not published until 1704 and the first volume of Bishop Burnet's not until 1724, though the first volume of Burnet's well known *History of the Reformation* appeared in 1681. The bibliographical sections of the *Cambridge Modern History* show that there was a sudden outburst of historical publications after 1700—histories of single reigns and single periods, memoirs, state documents, works relating to the reign of Elizabeth, the Civil War, the Revolution, the wars of the Pretenders, and even the American colonies. The titles of these works prove that history in our modern sense arose out of partisanship. The partisan tone still prevailed in the first great historical work of the century, Hume's *History of England* (Vol. I, 1754). Robertson's *History of Scotland* appeared in 1759. The first volume of Gibbon's *Rome* did not appear until 1776, but the researches on which it was based were begun at least ten years before. Gibbon was the only one of the three historians whose work was based on adequate research and therefore his history is the only one that has survived as an authority. Though their subjects and their personalities were so different, all three historians were men of their century. In spite of partisanship they had a critical regard for the truth. Though there is failure to see and to recognize some of the deeper forces operating in history, yet they tried to show the relation between events and there is a degree of social and political philosophy underlying the work of all three. They were all influenced by the chief writers of their times on historical theory, Bolingbroke, Montesquieu, and Voltaire[1], and their work was done or well begun by 1770, the date ending the period considered in this study of the historical point of view in literary criticism.

That the development in historical theory and practice just discussed was a necessary forerunner or accompaniment of the development in the application of the historical point of view in literary criticism, is a statement that needs only to be made to be accepted. It is only with the knowledge of that historical environment which history alone can give that such a point of view can be applied to literature at all. At the same time history itself can furnish the best examples of the application of the genetic method, while historical theory furnishes those precepts as to aims and methods most easily transferred to the field of literary study. The great increase of collected historical material from 1570 to 1770, the growth of historical writing as an art based on philosophical principles, and the increased discussion of these principles, were, then, all of direct importance in the development of the historical point of view in literary criticism, because they furnished necessary knowledge, examples and precepts.

---

[1] Cf. on the place of Hume, Robertson and Gibbon in the development of historiography, Grant, work cited, pp. xxxi—xxxvi, and Stephen, work cited, I. 57—58.

## 7. Summary.

I have attempted so far to clear the ground for the study of the English critical documents themselves. I have stated my purpose and pointed out the incentive to such a study because of the comparatively slight treatment the subject has received by the authorities on English criticism. I have tried to make clear why the limits of my study were placed at 1770, to discriminate between the different points of view in literary criticism, to show what is meant by the historical point of view, to sketch the background of influential foreign critical utterances, during the period considered, and to take a glance at the development of theory and practice in history proper which accompanied the growth of the historical point of view in literary criticism.

This introductory discussion ought to have made clear that in the three following chapters, taking up in order Elizabethan Criticism, Seventeenth Century Criticism and Eighteenth Century Criticism before 1770, what must be looked for is a recognition, directly, or indirectly, of some phase of a "relative aesthetic varying from age to age, from country to country".[1] Such a recognition may take the form of a denial of dogmatism, traditional or rationalistic, because aesthetic principles must vary from country to country, from age to age. Such criticism may insist on the right of national individuality in art, a right which will mean not merely a patriotic appreciation of the critic's own national literature, but also an increased tolerance for the literary art of other nations. It may demand that no standards of a past age shall rule the literature of the

[1] Cf. above, p. 18.

critic's own age, but this demand may be accompanied by a fuller and more sympathetic understanding of the literature of past ages. These various phases of the expression of such a relative aesthetic will be based on an implicit or more or less consciously expressed recognition of the unity and the continuity of national and community life, a recognition of the interwoven historical forces influencing literature, a recognition of the necessity of taking such forces into account in passing judgment upon a piece of literature or in arriving at any true appreciation of its worth.

---

# II. Elizabethan Criticism.[1]

## 1. Origin of Elizabethan Criticism and General Grouping of the Critics.

Elizabethan Criticism is almost wholly the result of attacks on English poetry by reformers and of answers to these attacks.[2] The attack was two-fold: first, on moral grounds, against the immoral tendencies in the contemporary acted drama, and against the same tendencies in the still popular native medieval romances and in contemporary lyric poetry, and finally against foreign influences, especially Italian, in poetry and romance; and, second, on literary grounds, against the prevailing verse forms in English poetry and impure style in the language.

The moral attack, so far as those who wrote wholly from the moral standpoint are concerned, was against various kinds of public entertainers and entertainments; poetry and drama were not the only offenders.[3] In regard to poetry, part of their attack was at once taken over by the humanists and used for their own purposes. We are not concerned with the moral attack when made wholly

[1] Unless otherwise noted, the references to critical texts will be to those found in Gregory Smith's *Elizabethan Critical Essays.*

[2] Cf. Smith, I. xiv ff., and Spingarn, *Lit. Crit. in the Ren.*, p. 257.

[3] Cf. titles of reforming pamphlets to 1587, Smith, I. 61—63.

by moralists; it is only when this becomes part of the humanist propaganda, or inspires the defense of poetry, that a student of criticism becomes interested. It must be remembered that Ascham, More and the earlier men of the New Learning were all reformers, that they were reformers in church and state as well as in literature; but their whole point of view was aristocratic. They wished to reform from above downward; they wanted no cataclysmic revolution, but desired the truth gradually to permeate the unleavened mass below, if that were possible, through the efforts of the divinely appointed leaders above. They and their later followers were in earnest in their denunciation of the corrupt moral elements in literature. Smith has pointed out, however, that the foes of poetry and the defenders did not meet on exactly common ground (I. xx). The Puritans, in the main, were men of the people and were thinking only of popular literature and popular stage entertainments. The defenders were university men, scholars and courtiers, who, on the whole, despised the popular literature and were perfectly willing to grant its viciousness and even to out-Herod Herod in its denunciation. Their defense, then, is based on the value of a different kind of poetry from that the Puritans had in mind. This is one part of the explanation why, in general, Elizabethan critics failed to discuss adequately the great national literature then beginning to spring up around them. Another reason for this failure is that the better national literature was still to be produced when the mass of Elizabethan criticism was written, and the larger body of popular literature open to discussion when the Elizabethan critics began to write deserved the contempt they gave it.

The grouping of the Elizabethan critics under the different banners shows that sometimes a man must be counted on both sides. Ascham began the moral attack as a humanist in 1570. He was followed by the great protagonist of the Puritans, Gosson. Later critics, like Whetstone, Meres and Vaughan, follow up the moral attack in part, while the defenders of poetry, like Sidney, Puttenham and Harrington, were, in a degree, sympathetic toward the moral ideals of the Puritans. In fact, the whole list of defenders, Lodge, Sidney, Stanyhurst, Webbe, Puttenham, Nash, Harrington, use the moral value of poetry as one of their arguments. Even Vaughan, who condemns stage plays, argues in behalf "Of Poetry and of the excellency there of" (II. 309), while Meres who had black-listed the medieval romances, believed that there are "many things very profitable to be known" in poetry (II. 325 f.).

The literary attack also had sufficient reason for its beginning. The early reformers were in favor of the use of English as against Latin, but they realized that English as a language needed to set its house in order. Latinists and humanists as they were, they fought against ink-horn terms of whatever origin, whether French-English, English Italianated or Latin.[1] The Elizabethans believed in the powers and possibilities of their language, and worked patriotically to improve it. Saintsbury has pointed out why the second literary reform, the attempt to make over English prosody, came into being.[2] No one of the three forms in

[1] Cf. Wilson's *Art of Rhetorique* (1553) in Saintsbury's *Loci Critici*, pp. 89—90; also, Ascham's *Scholemaster* (Arber), pp. 111—112; and Gascoigne, I. 51.

[2] *Hist. of Crit.*, II. 157—160. Cf. Schelling's *Poetic and Verse Criticism*, p. 4ff.

use then—the Chaucerian, the Alliterative and the Italianated, as Saintsbury calls them—could be considered by their performances in Ascham's time as satisfactory; and hence naturally arose a movement—coming first from St. John's College, Cambridge—to put matters right in the only way the scholars of the New Learning could conceive of, by imitating classical meters. This attack of the critics was inevitable; and the defense against the remedy proposed culminated in the one critical work where the historical point of view was given any adequate expression in the Elizabethan period, Daniel's *Defence of Ryme.*

The movement for the application of classical principles to English poetry was led by Ascham and numbered among its adherents on the various subjects included —classical measures *vs.* rhyme, and the unities and decorum in the drama—Ascham himself, Whetstone, Spenser, Harvey, "E. K.", Stanyhurst, Sidney, Webbe, and Campion.[1] The defenders of the national tradition in poetry —the battle over the drama was to be fought out later— included, first, Gascoigne and King James, who were for the defense by implication, rather than by explicit statement. The former's *Certayne Notes of Instruction* and the latter's *Reulis and Cautelis* assumed that the system inherited from Chaucer, as modified by Surrey and Wyatt after their Italian models, was the correct system for English verse. Sidney believed that English was "fit for both sorts" of versifying.[2] Puttenham dallied with classical

---

[1] Cf. also the extract from the unknown author of the "Preservation of King Henry the VII", Smith, I. 377—8, and Blenerhasset's *Induction*, Schelling, p. 23f.

[2] I. 204—205. But Spenser claimed that Sidney was responsible for perfecting Drant's scheme (I. 99).

verse forms, but he had no doubt of the superiority of the traditional English verse forms; the use of classical measures he considered purely an academic question (II. 134). Nash ridiculed "Hexameter" Harvey's attempts, but Harvey himself could not go so far as to accept the complete classical "Dranting" of English verse.[1] Whether the "Areopagus" was wholly in earnest or not in its attempt to banish rhyme and the national system of verse, is open to doubt.[2] There are at least grounds for suspicion that Sidney and Spenser and Dyer were not much more serious than was that other courtier, Puttenham, when he was toying with classical measures. The tone of the Spenser-Harvey letters is strangely light for serious reformers (I. 87—126), and Spenser was earnestly at work all the time on the "Faerye Queene" and other English verses. Campion appears to have been in earnest, temporarily, at least, little as we can conceive of it in connection with his own poetry; but neither he, nor Stanyhurst, nor Harvey, nor even Ascham himself, believed that the prosodic rules of one language could be applied wholly to another. We can at least be grateful for the fad, if it was no more than that among the later men, for it gave Daniel the occasion he needed for the defense of the national tradition.

## 2. Possibilities for the Period.

Even a cursory reading of Elizabethan criticism will make it evident that the larger number of the critics were

---

[1] Cf. I. 119, 121; II. 272.

[2] Cf. Maynadier, *The Areopagus of Sidney and Spenser, Mod. Lang. Rev.* IV. 289—301. For the opposite view, see Fletcher, *Areopagus and Pléiade, Jour. Eng. & Germ. Phil.* II. 429—453.

almost wholly without the true historical sense and point of view. It could hardly be expected that they could have it. It had as yet been expressed neither in criticism nor in history itself. Bodin seemed to be practically unknown. The method of the defense of poetry against the Puritan attack was outlined in advance in the attack itself. The opponents of the Puritans and still more the aristocracy of birth and learning for whom they really wrote, would listen to only one kind of defence. Along with their direct onslaught on the immorality of poetry as everybody knew it, the Puritans used the argument of authority and piled up testimony of supposedly expert witnesses like the church fathers and Plato. The defenders had to retort by piling up more authority, showing the long descent of poetry, its early sacred character, its allegorical teaching power, the favor of the great, etc. It hardly need be said that the argument from authority is not in keeping with the historical point of view. The better chance to use the historical method came with the opportunity to defend the national literary tradition, but most of the critics, Daniel excepted, were either on the other side or devoted their strength to answering the Puritan attack. The earlier reformers in matters literary could not well be otherwise than classical in intention. They felt that the language and its poetic forms must be subjected to the discipline of art, and the only literary art they knew or could respect was found in the classics. As has been pointed out[1], no one before Campion and Daniel could well have written with any full realization that the national tradition could justify itself in practice, for no other important Elizabethan

---

[1] *Supra*, p. 38.

critic at the time of writing had seen the great achievements of Shakespeare and his greater contemporaries.[1]

As has been already suggested, any attempt at a careful classification of the Elizabethan critics is bound to meet with difficulties. The authorities on the history of criticism do not agree on the matter. Hamelius, for example, has only two large periods in the whole sixteenth and seventeenth centuries. The first reaches to the Commonwealth and this he divides into two parts, Renaissance criticism before Jonson, and Jonson's foundation of the Neo-classic school.[2] Gayley and Scott have only one period from Ascham to Bacon, a period they characterize as "Chiefly Theoretical and Largely Academic".[3] Spingarn in his *Literary Criticism in the Renaissance* offers a more minute division. The first, down to and including Ascham, is devoted to the "purely rhetorical study of literature". The second, from Gascoigne to the *Defenses*, is a period of classification and of metrical studies. The third, from Sidney to Daniel, is the period of philosophical and apologetic criticism (pp. 254 ff.). Spingarn's division is in a broad way chronological, and in a general way corresponds to the change in critical thought. Yet there are so many cross-currents that even so simple and broad a classification as this is likely to suffer from inconsistencies. The easiest way for a further discussion of Elizabethan criticism in this study is to take the various critics up chronologically and to show not only the cross currents in each individual but also what development there may be in time sequence.

---

[1] Cf. for this paragraph, Smith, I. xiv—xvi, and Spingarn, *Lit. Crit. in Ren.*, pp. 296—310.

[2] *Die Kritik in der Eng. Lit.*, p. 7 ff.

[3] *Lit. Crit.*, pp. 389 ff.

Two things in the following examination of the different Elizabethan critics may call for explanation. The first of these is that some space is given up to a negative task, to a statement of critical utterances opposed to the historical point of view. Such a procedure can justify itself only because the Elizabethans wrought in a time of beginnings, in the formative period, and while their absolute value as a group is considerably less than that of later critics, their relative importance is increased because they do represent this period of origins. Hence all that they said, against as well as for the historical point of view, deserves some notice. The carrying out of this principle involves, then, the devotion of more space to the Elizabethan critics than as a group, always excepting Daniel, they can possibly deserve intrinsically.

## 3. Chronological Discussion of Individual Critics.

Ascham, the first important Elizabethan critic in point of time, is in many ways typical of the period. The *Scholemaster* (1570) contains much material valuable to the student of criticism. He insists, in the first place, that if anything good is to be found in any of the modern languages, or even in Latin, "Cicero onelie excepted, . . . it is either lerned, borrowed, or stolne, from those worthy wittes of Athens".[1] God's wise providence destroyed their contemporaries, but saved Plato, Aristotle and Tullie to serve as models to after times, and any man who will love and follow them will be "learned, wise and also an honest man", provided he adds the Bible.[2] He believes that excellence in a language goes with good moral con-

[1] *Scholemaster* (Arber), p. 60. — [2] I. 7; cf. pp. 22, 29.

duct in the nation (pp. 6, 27), but such perfection in language cannot last longer than a century, "for no perfection is durable" (p. 26)—a principle that ought to have suggested the inconsistency of setting up any absolute standard. His well known attack on "rude beggerly ryming, brought first into Italie by *Gothes* and *Hunnes,* whan all good verses and all good learning to were destroyed by them, and after caryd into France and Germanie, and at last receyued into England" (pp. 29—35), contains in this sentence the view, still orthodox in the eighteenth century, that learning and art and civilization are always consciously destroyed, or imported or fostered, as the case may be. He has no conception of natural and more or less unconscious growth of the arts. His system of imitation is to be a conscious art, and the very word "art" in literary criticism comes to mean for the next two hundred years this deliberate study and imitation of models and conscious application of rules. Ascham weakens his case by acknowledging the force of "tyme and custome" in sanctifying rhyme and that the very nature of the English tongue makes it practically impossible to use all the classical measures (p. 30). His standard is wholly aristocratic—the author should rather satisfy one learned man than please a multitude (p. 31). His hatred of both medieval and Italian romances is not wholly from the Puritan and Protestant standpoint, though he attributes the introduction of Italian romances to "secrete Papistes" and had a due Protestant contempt for "idle Monkes and wanton Chanons"; as a matter of fact, he had the classicist's contempt for the ignorance and formlessness of medieval literature and for the lawlessness of Italian romance, what we now call its romantic art, a contempt taught him, directly or indirectly, by the orthodox Italian humanists.[1] The only things in Ascham that might be mentioned as tending toward the historical point of view are his intense patriotism, and his quotation from Cheke, analyzing Sallust's style and accounting for its likeness to the style of Thucydides and its difference from the styles of Caesar and Cicero partly through the influence of environment (pp. 40—43). This last is confessedly not his own, and so Ascham can well stand as the father of dogmatic criticism.

Some of the critics from Ascham to Daniel deserve but passing notice. In Gascoigne's *Certayne Notes of Instruction* (1575), meant, as I have suggested[2], to be merely a practical manual, there is nothing to interest us, except his reverence for Chaucer (I. 47, 50, 56). Blenerhasset's appeal against the "Gotish" kind of rhyming and for "Roman verse" (1577) is merely an early echo of Ascham.[3] Whetstone's Dedication to *Promos and Cassandra* (1578) is noteworthy only for its full statement of the classical principle of decorum. He attacks the lewdness of the French and Italian drama and makes the first effective statement of the irregularity of the English drama (I. 58—60). Sidney follows him in this and later the rationalists, Davenant, Hobbes, Rymer and others, develop his doctrine of decorum. Lodge had the honor of writing in 1579 the first *Defence of Poetry,* a chaotic piece, but it blocked out the lines of the later "Defences". Lodge cites his authorities wholly from the classics, though Chaucer is used once as an example (I. 69), and the only

[1] Smith, I. xxi; cf. Spingarn, *Lit. Crit. in the Ren.*, pp. 254—255.

[2] *Supra*, p. 40. — [3] Schelling, pp. 23—24.

faint intimation of the historical standpoint, is a "suppose" that English actors "drew ther plaies and fourme of garments" from the Romans (I. 83). "E. K's." *Epistle Dedicatory to the Shepheards Calendar* (1579), addressed in flattering terms to Harvey, praises Chaucer and commends Spenser for decorum, use of old words and following the example of the "most ancient Poetes", and condemns with due scholarly and courtier-like contempt the "rakehellye route of our ragged rymers" (I. 128—131).

Up to the Spenser-Harvey correspondence (1579—1580), then, there is practically no trace of the historical point of view. This whole correspondence shows that Harvey is far from deserving the conventional sneers bestowed upon him for his supposed pedantry. The probability is that literary historians and biographers have felt it necessary to declare that the two amiable and popular young poets, Sidney and Spenser, were led astray by Harvey, and have so declared without proper investigation.[1] We do not have the least evidence that Drant's rules or practice could have "fired Harvey to be a reformer", as Smith suggests (I. 1). In the first letter Spenser declares he has been drawn to the faction of Sidney and Dyer, in their "surceasing and silence of balde Rymers . . . insteade whereof, they haue, by the authoritie of their whole Senate, prescribed certaine Laws and rules of Quantities of English Sillables for English Verse", and that he is already using Drant's rules to judge attempts at classical verse (I. 89—90). In answer Harvey refuses to accept Drant's rules as authority because "My selfe neither sawe them, nor heard of them before" (p. 97). Then Spenser asks why English cannot make accent depend upon quan-

[1] Cf. Schelling, *Poetic and Verse Criticism,* pp. 24—28.

tity as well as Greek and asserts that Sidney worked over and expanded Drant's rules (p. 98). Harvey's answer says he does not dare lay down rules (pp. 102—103), and that Spenser should not dare to change the accent against "generall receyued Custome", for "the Latin is no rule for us" (pp. 117—118). It is a classicist with decidedly good sense who asserts: "We are not to go a little farther, either for the *Prosody* or the *Orthography* . . . then we are licenced and authorized by the ordinarie use, and custome, and proprietie, and Idiome, and, as it were, Maiestie of our speach: which I accounte the only infallible and soueraigne Rule of all Rules" (p. 119). He further declares: "It is the vulgare and naturall Mother *Prosodye*, that alone worketh the feate, as the onely supreame Foundresse and Reformer of Position, Dipthong, Orthographie, or whatsoever else: whose Affirmatives are nothing worth, if she once conclude the Negative", and he finally refuses to give any "Artificial Rules and Precepts" (pp. 121—122). Though in his defense against Greene Harvey says, "let me rather be epitaphed, The Inventor of the English Hexameter", he means, than be the author of Greene's works (II. 230—231); this "epitaph" is part of a defense, and those who quote it generally misrepresent Harvey. The passages above make it evident that a man who saw so clearly the foolishness of Sidney's and Spenser's "Dranting"[1] and who stated such a "Rule of Rules" was well on the way, in this particular, at least, toward the historical standpoint. It must be confessed that he never wholly reached it.

Stanyhurst's *Dedication* and *Preface* to his *Æneid* (1582) and his translation itself, show that he followed

[1] Harvey condemns "Dranting" again in 1593. See II. 272.

Harvey's principles in verse reform rather than Drant's and Sidney's. He also approaches the historical standpoint in his statement of fundamental principles, and shows Harvey's liberality in disdaining to make rules for others. He says definitely that he was trying to carry out Ascham's ideas.[1] But he knows that Latin quantity is no exact rule for English and gets at the principle that would destroy any rigid classical verse scheme for English when he says, "For the final eend of a verse is too please thee eare". Then on the same page he attacks "these grammatical Precisians" with the notable statement that, "as every countrye hath his peculiar law, so they permit euerye language too vse his particular loore" (I. 141—142). His refusal to make rules for others shows the characteristic open-mindedness of some of the Elizabethan classicists[2], while the sentence just quoted contains the gist of Daniel's argument from the historical point of view.

Sidney's *Apologie* (1581—1583) deserves its fame for what Schelling calls "its lofty ideality"[3]; for us it does not present much. Sidney soon deserted "Dranting". In the *Apologie* he devotes but two paragraphs to the two kinds of versifying, and arrives at the patriotic but reasoned conclusion that, "Truely the English, before any other vulgar language I know, is fit for both sorts" (I. 204—205); and then he proceeds to show why. On the other technical problem, so widely discussed in the next two centuries, the question of the dramatic unities, Sidney ranges himself on the side of "Aristotle's precept and common reason",[4] and in this phrase sums up the text for the

[1] I. 137. Harvey, too, mentions Ascham with respect: cf. I. 102, 118, 120. — [2] Cf. Smith, I. xxxix—xl.

[3] Work cited, p. 76. — [4] p. 197; cf. 196—201.

future discussion. This is the only section of the *Apologie* where Sidney shows himself an out-and-out classicist, but that he should follow Whetstone in condemning the English popular drama of 1581—1583, not yet emancipated from the formlessness of the miracle plays, is not inexcusable. Yet in his love for ballads (I. 178) and praise of romances (pp. 173, 179, 188), in his discussion of style and the English language (pp. 201—204), in his recognition of genius before "art" (p. 195), he is even more tolerant than the majority of his contemporaries. In one brief instance only does he use the historical method, and that is where he accounts for the nature of Pindar's poetry as the result of "the tyme and custome of the Greekes".[1]

In his *Schort Treatise* (1584) King James states in the *Preface* why he has written the treatise, when so many others have already written on the subject. His first reason is that Scotch is not English, and though English "is lykest to our language, yit we differ from thame in sindrie reulis of Poesie, as ye will find be experience" (I. 209) — a direct statement of difference in national standards. The chief reason for writing, however, is that the rules for Poesie must necessarily change with time— "lyke as the tyme is changeit sensyne, sa is the ordour of Poesie changeit", and he speaks optimistically of Poesie, "as being come to mannes age and perfectioun, quhair as then it was bot in the infancie and chyldheid" (I. 209). Moreover, he knows one must have genius before rules are worth anything (p. 210). The statement of his two reasons above is sufficient to rank him as the first English critic—I beg his pardon, for he is certainly Scotch!—to

[1] p. 179. Sidney preceded Chapman, Milton and others in praise of the Bible as literature (158).

bring definitely together two fundamental principles of the historical method: (1) that the literary standards of one nation cannot apply directly to the work of another; and (2) that in the same nation standards must vary from period to period. Still the *Treatise* that follows is only a re-hash of Gascoigne.

In the full title of Webbe's *Discourse of English Poetrie* (1586), the second part—*Together with the Author's iudgment, touching the reformation of English Verse*—indicates where Webbe is likely to stand on the question of classical meters. He blames the English barbarousness in poetry upon the "cankered enmitie of curious custome" (I. 228). Still he offers a bit of alternative to his classical *Prosodia* for English—"where it would skant abyde the touch of theyr Rules" he is willing to establish new rules "by the naturall affectation of the speeche" (p. 229). Later he quotes Ascham on the origin of "this brutish Poetrie . . . this tinkerly verse which we call ryme" (p. 240). Yet the poor fellow "may not utterly dissalowe it, least I should seeme to call in question the iudgement of all our famous wryters, which haue wonne eternall prayse by theyr memorable workes compyled in that verse" (p. 266), and anyway English rhymes are better than any other! As a matter of fact Webbe has nothing but a naive working over of other men's material, and would hardly deserve the space above had he not himself given considerable space to brief and pretty crude appreciations of various English poets—his "simple judgment", as he rightly calls it (pp. 240—247).

There is nothing in the summary Smith gives of Fraunce's *Arcadian Rhetorike* (I. 303—306) (1588) to have us pause, and so we can pass on to the man Schelling calls "Harvey's natural enemy"[1], Thomas Nash. Smith includes four selections from Nash — the *Preface* to *Menaphon* and the *Anatomie of Absurditie* (both 1589) in Volume I, and the *Preface* to *Astrophel and Stella* (1591) and *Strange Newes* (1592) in Volume II. Nash is, on the whole, distinctly for the Moderns, and for the more recent Moderns, as against the "Abbie-lubbers" and their Arthurian and other medieval romances (I. 323). He is quite sure of the superiority of the English poets from Chaucer to Spenser over all comers (pp. 318—320). He exploits the "extemporall vaine", the original genius, of his own school of University Wits, over "our greatest Art-masters deliberate thoughts" (p. 309), that is, he praises original genius at the expense of the rules long before Young. He pokes fun at Stanyhurst's "hexameter furie", and later, in his reply to Harvey, exposes the shallow reasoning of those who advocate the classical verse. "Hexamiter verse", he says, "I graunt to be a Gentleman of an auncient house (so is many an English begger); yet this Clyme of ours he cannot thriue in . . . *Homer and Virgil, two valorous Authors*, yet were they never knighted, they wrote in Hexameter Verses: *Ergo, Chaucer* and *Spenser*, the *Homer* and *Virgil* of England, were farre ouerseene that they wrote not all their Poems in Hexamiter verses also. In many Countries veluet and Satten is a commoner weare than cloth amongst vs: Ergo, wee must leaue wearing of cloth, and goe euerie one in veluet and satten, because other Countries vse so . . . *Our english tongue is nothing too good, but* too bad *to imitate the Greeke and Latine*" (II. 240). Nash really believes in the national

---

[1] Work cited, p. 37.

tradition and in the new English literature and is less cumbered with the "Ancients" than any man we have met before.

Puttenham's *Arte of English Poesie* (1589) is large enough to be called a treatise. But we don't dare to call it that, since his aim was wholly popular—to make this Art vulgar "for all Englishmens use". "I write to the pleasure of a Lady [Elizabeth herself] . . . and neither to Priests nor to Prophets or Philosophers" (II. 25 and 193). In other words, Puttenham is writing for the public, for the same public Dryden addresses, for "society", and not for an aristocracy of scholars; his book was intentionally "fitter to please the Court than the schoole" (pp. 164—165). He has succeeded in writing a *vade mecum* for those who would "become good makers in the vulgar", or for those who would "iudge of other mens makings" (p. 165). The "arte" of his title means "a certaine order of rules prescribed by reason, and gathered by experience"; that is, he excludes authority and insists, therefore, that Poesie may be "a vulgar Art with vs as well as with the Greeks and Latines" (p. 5). On the vexed question of poetical measures, he is wholly in favor of accentual verse and rhyme. His argument in favor of rhyme is so explicit that it must have influenced Daniel. He cites the whole world, from the Hebrews and Chaldees to the American Indians and "the vary Canniball", to prove that "our maner of vulgar Poesie is more ancient then the artificiall of the Greeks and Latines, ours coming by instinct of nature, which was before Art or Observation, and used with the savage and vnciuill, who were before all science or ciuilitie" (p. 10—11). This whole chapter is worth reading, because it is not only one of Daniel's strongest arguments, but also involves the material Brown worked on in 1764. Puttenham knew classical measures were merely "friuolous and rediculous", and that "custome" alone could fix any art of poetry (pp. 124—130). He explains the treatment of the heathen gods in ancient poetry by the character of the oriental princes in the likeness of whom they had been created (pp. 29—40). Puttenham is, then, sane and modern, and to a certain extent historical in his outlook.

Harrington's *Brief Apologie* (1591) is in three parts —he apologizes for poetry, for Ariosto and for his own translation. In the first he quotes Sidney and Puttenham and evidently follows them. The third we need not consider. In the second he tries Ariosto by the *Æneid* as a model and by the rules of Aristotle as an authority. But this subserviency to dogmatism is tempered somewhat. An answer to one objection of the "rules" is, "Methinks it is a sufficient defence to say, *Ariosto* doth it" (II. 217), that is, he sets up a modern against the ancients on the principle that good work needs no excuse from precedent. Again against those who reduce "all heroicall Poems vnto the methode of *Homer* and certain precepts of *Aristotle*", he replies, "for Homer I say that that which was commendable in him to write in that age, the times being changed, would be thought otherwise now" (pp. 215—216). That each author has the right to be judged on the merits of his own performance, and that standards change with the age, are principles which ought to rank Harrington high on the question of fixed external standards, but unfortunately most of his space is given up to a direct acknowledgment and application of dogmatic standards.

The next productions chronologically, Nash's essays in Smith's second volume, have been noticed above[1], and the same is true of all that concerns us in Harvey's later essays[2],—Foure Letters (1592), *Pierces Supererogation* and *A New Letter of Notable Contents* (1593). The next essay, Carew's *The Excellency of the English Tongue* (1593), asserts that English has gathered all the good qualities of all the other modern languages and escaped their faults (II. 292—243), a mark of the Elizabethan critical patriotism, but he gives more proof than Sidney did.[3] Yet Carew believes rules may be applied deductively, and he is not entirely in favor of establishing something "by nature or by Custome", or by the "antiquitye from our Elders and the universalitye of our neighbours" (p. 285), and hence could hardly accept reasoning like Puttenham's on rhyme.

Chapman's *Preface* to his *Iliad* and his *Dedication* to *Achilles Shield* (1598) are chiefly remarkable for his magnificent defense of Homer against "soule-blind" Scaliger's exaltation of Vergil at the expense of Homer (II. 301). Chapman's own teaching is an exaltation of original genius over talent guided by rules or models. "*Homers* Poems", he says, "were writ from a free furie, an absolute and full soule, Virgils out of a courtly, laborious, and altogether imitatorie spirit" (p. 298)—a sentence that has in it the possibility of dissolving the whole neo-classic fabric of rules and imitation and that contains the essence of Young's essay in 1759. Yet the assertion of the necessity for original genius is far from uncommon

---

[1] *Supra*, pp. 52—53. — [2] *Supra*, pp. 47—48.
[3] Cf. I. 204—205.

among the Elizabethans[1], though the contrast is more strongly expressed here. Still Chapman's praise for genius contributes only indirectly to the development of the historical point of view. Fortunately he can be quoted directly against the craze for classical measures—

> "Sweet Poesy
> Will not be clad in her supremacy
> With those strange garments (Rome's hexameters),
> As she is English." [2]

Mere's *Palladis Tamia* (1598) offers us nothing, except his condemnation of the long list of medieval romances (II. 308). In 1599 appeared another brief plea for English hexameters and pentameters by some "Anon" in an address to the "Reader" prefixed to the *First Booke of the Preservation of King Henry the VII*,[3] certainly a belated plea. Vaughan's *Golden Grove* (1600) shows him opposed to the abuses of poetry and a contemner of all "stage playes", but a defender of "true" poetry.[4]

Why Campion should write his *Observations in the Art of English Poesie* as late as 1602, and why he wrote it at all, is hard to explain today; the attempt at classical verse had practically ceased, and he himself was a pastmaster in the native verse forms.[5] It would hardly be worth while to quote his arguments or the details of his system, were it not that they furnished Daniel his excuse for his *Defence*. Campion opens with the hackneyed account of how "Learning first flourished in *Greece*; from

---

[1] Cf. Lodge, I. 71; Sidney, I. 195; Nash, I. 309; Puttenham, II. 3; Harrington, II. 197.

[2] Quoted by Smith, I. liv.

[3] See Smith's note, I. 377—378.

[4] Cf. the summary by Smith, II. 325—326.

[5] Cf. Smith, I. xlvii and xlix.

thence it was derived vnto the Romaines", and goes on to tell how the Barbarians deformed Learning, how Erasmus, Rewcline and More rescued Latin out of the hands of "illiterate Monks and Friers", and that "In those lack-learning times, and in barbarized Italy", rhyme began (II. 329). This is the old story, familiar since Ascham. Campion recognizes what he has to contend against, the age-old custom and the "consent of many nations", and he is too much the artist not to see the "passing pitifull success" of the attempts at English hexameters, and besides it was "altogether against the nature of our language" (pp. 330, 333). His system, therefore, is not "Dranting"; he follows more the common-sense ideas of Harvey and Puttenham. After all his own attempt is not so radical as that of Sidney and Spenser.

Daniel's answer to Campion, *A Defence of Ryme*, was not written until 1603.[1] How far he secured material from his predecessors can be easily answered. He could not have secured much, because there was not much to secure. He was probably familiar with all the previous critical literature, and may have received hints from Stanyhurst and Nash and Harrington. He probably got suggestions from King James[2], and certainly did from

[1] Smith places a question mark before this date (II. 356) and says in his note (II. 457) that it might be 1602. Schelling (p. 84), Gayley and Scott (p. 390), and Child (*Cam. Eng. Lit.*, IV. 133) say 1602. Dates are sometimes important, and as the result of an investigation of the original editions, I propose to publish soon a note on this particular date.

[2] Cf. I. 209. At the very time of writing the *Defence* Daniel was paying special compliments to James and his family. He complimented the queen of James as early as 1602, sent a "Panegyrike Congratulatory" to James on his way to London in 1603 and complimented him again in the second paragraph of his *Defence* (p. 357).

Puttenham.[1] That he knew the literature of the subject well is made clear by his definite citation of Tolomei as the originator of the movement for classical measures in modern times[2], and his proved use of Giraldi Cintio's *Discorso dei Romanzi*[3], in which, according to Spingarn, "Italian literature is for the first time critically distinguished from classical literature in regard to language, religion, and nationality".[4] Probably one definite influence was his own long continued work on his patriotic poem, the *Civil Wars*, the first part of which was published as early as 1595 and the last two books as late as 1609.[5] He was recognized as a special student in the history of his own country and in 1609 he says "many noble and worthy spirits" were urging him to write a large English history, and he actually published such a history in 1612—1617. His interest in history and especially in the history of his own country is certainly a suggestive influence upon the *Defence*.

Important as the whole essay is, I shall mention here only the chief points. Daniel is not much concerned over Campion's purely metrical schemes. The first phrase in the essay shows what the foundation of his argument is: "The Generall Custome and vse of Ryme in this Kingdom, Noble Lord, hauing been so long (as if from a Graunt of Nature) held unquestionable" (II. 357). Therefore he wrote rhymes "perceiving it agreed so well, both with the complexion of the times and mine own constitution".[6] Then comes his main thesis against Campion: "We could well

---

[1] Cf. the whole of Ch. V., pp. 10—11, in Vol. II.

[2] p. 368. Cf. Spingarn, *Lit. Crit. in the Ren.*, p. 126.

[3] II. 360, l. 16 and note, p. 458. — [4] *Lit. Crit. in Ren.*, p. 163.

[5] Cf. Hamelius, p. 19, and *supra*, p. 31.

[6] p. 358. Note that this is both psychological and historical.

have allowed of his numbers, had he not disgraced our Ryme, which both Custome and Nature doth most powerfully defend: Custome that is before all law, Nature that is before all Arte. Every language hath her proper number or measure fitted to vse and delight, which Custome intertaininge by the allowance of the Eare, doth indenize and make naturall" (p. 359).

To prove his thesis, he first distinguishes between classical verse and the English verse form, repeating Puttenham's argument that English verse has all necessary parts of classic verse, "number, measure and harmonie in the best proportion of music", and that modern verse is superior to ancient verse because it has the added "Harmonie" of rhyme, "giving both to the Eare an Echo of a delightful report, and to the memorie a deeper impression of what is delivered therein".[1] Then to prove the "Custom before all Law", and "Nature above all Arte", he asserts the universality of rhyme[2], for Asia, Africa and all Europe (p. 361). It cannot be called "an ill custome which nature has thus ratified, all nations received, time so long confirmed, the effects such as it performes those officies of motion for which it is employed; delighting the eare, stirring the heart, and satisfying the iudgement in such sort as I doubt whether euer single numbers will doe in our Climate" (p. 362).

This statement of the value of rhyme leads directly to his statement of the principle on which delight must depend. "And if euer they proove to become anything", he goes on, "it must be by the approbation of many ages that must give them their strength for any operation,

[1] p. 360. See for the superiority of modern stanzaic structure, p. 366. — [2] Cf. Puttenham, *supra*, p. 53.

as before when the world will feel where the pulse, life and enargie lies" (p. 362). But not only must there be long use to give delight, the poetic form to produce this delight varies with different nations. Hence his conclusion: "Suffer then the world to enjoy that which it knows, and what it likes: Seeing that whatsoever force of words doth moue, delight, and sway the affections of men, in what Scythian sorte soeuer it be disposed or uttered, that is true number, measure, eloquence, and the perfection of speech: which I said hath as many shapes as there be tongues or nations in the world, nor can with all the tyrannical Rules of idle Rhetorique be governed otherwise than custome and present observation will allow" (p. 363).

If delight must vary for different nations, it follows logically that no nation has the right to prescribe poetic rules for another. Daniel can even find specific fault with classical methods in versification and says that the Greeks and Latins "may thank their sword that made their tongues so famous and universall as they are" (p. 364). And then comes the positive Declaration of Independence: "all our understandings are not to be built by the square of *Greece* and *Italie.* We are the children of nature as well as they . . . the same Sunne of Discretion shineth uppon us . . . It is not bookes, but only that great booke of the world and the all-overspreading grace of heaven that makes men truly iudicial" (pp. 366—367).

This leads to the principle of historical tolerance: "Nor can it be but a touch of arrogant ignorance to hold this or that nation Barbarous, these or those times grosse, considering how this manifold creature man, wheresoeuer hee stand in the world, hath always some disposition of worth". The Greeks, then, were guilty of "presumptious errour", when they "held all other nations barbarous but themselues", which leads directly to a defense of the loudly scorned "*Gothes*, *Vandals*, and *Langobards*". They say, says Daniel, that the inundation of the "Barbarians" overwhelmed "all the glory of learning in Europe", but the "Barbarian laws and customs are the sources of most of the state constitutions in Europe", and all the testimony of those they conquered, "proues them not without iudgement, though without Greeke and Latine" (pp. 367—368). Even in Learning the despised Barbarians have proved themselves worthy. Because China never heard of Anapests and Tribrachs, she is not therefore gross and barbarous, and that unfortunate statement of Campion's about the "pittifully deformed" Learning before Rewcline, Erasmus, and More, is equally as ignorant as the assertion of the first would be. Petrarch alone disproves the whole thing and Tolomei's plea to copy the Ancients could never induce Tasso, "the wonder of Italy", to write in anything but his native verse, "that admirable Poem of *Jerusalem* comparable to the best of the Ancients" (p. 369). Then follows a long list of eminent Renaissance scholars who awakened the nations long before Campion's trio appeared, "worthy men, I confess, and the last [More] a great ornament to this land, and", he adds triumphantly, "a Rymer". He ends his defense of the Middle Ages by a list of learned men in England in the Dark Ages themselves, from Bede to Ockam (pp. 369—370). This analogical, historical argument reaches a climax in a tribute to his own country, which begins, "Let us go no further, but looke upon the wonderfull Architecture of this state of *England*, and see whether they were deformed times that could give it such a form" (pp. 372—373).

Before this last paragraph, however, comes the statement of another essential principle: "The distribution of giftes are uniuersall, and all seasons haue them in some part. We must not thinke but that there were *Scipioes*, *Caesars*, *Catoes* and *Pompeies* borne elsewhere then at *Rome*; the rest of the world hath ever had them in the same degree of nature, though not of state ... and in all ages, though they were not Ciceronians, they knew the Art of men, which only is the *Ars Artium*, the great gift of heauen, and the chief grace and glory on earth; they had the learning of Gouernement, and ordering their State; Eloquence inough to shew their iudgements" (p. 371). At last he reaches a statement that anticipates Vico and Montesquieu: "There is but one learning ... one and the selfe-same spirit that worketh in all. We have but one bodie of Iustice, one bodie of Wisdome thorowout the whole world; which is but apparalled according to the fashion of every nation" (p. 372).

The technical details of the controversy with Campion interest us here but little. He proves decisively that Campion's much heralded "new numbers", so far as they are conformable to the language, are "Onely what was our owne before, and the same but apparelled in forraine Titles" (p. 377). Daniel is perfectly willing to accept a reform, if it is in harmony with the genius of the language. He does not admire couplets and he believes so far with Campion, that "a Tragedie would indeede best comporte with a blank verse".

This confession of his own preferences leads him to the final statement of that "relative aesthetic, varying from age to age"[1]: "But in these things, I say, I dare not

[1] Cf. *supra*, pp. 18 and 35—36.

take upon mee to teach that they ought to be so, or that I think it right; for indeed there is no right in these things that are continually in a wandring motion, carried with the violence of uncertaine likings, being but only the time that gives them their power" (p. 383). He concludes the essay in a vein almost gloomily philosophical, when, speaking of another matter, his last sentence says, "But this is but a Character of that perpetuall reuolution which wee see to be in all things that neuer remain the same: and wee must heerein be content to submit ourselves to the law of time, which in few yeares wil make al that for which we now contend *Nothing*" (p. 384). Nevertheless the principles of a shifting standard of taste have at last been fully stated.

An examination of Daniel's *Defence of Ryme* cannot end better than in his own words: "And therefore heere I stand foorth, onelie to make good the place we have thus taken up, and to defend the sacred monuments erected therein, which containe the honour of the dead, the fame of the liuing, the glory of peace, and the best power of our speach, and wherein so many honourable spirits have sacrificed to Memorie their dearest passions, shewing by what diuine influence they have been moued and under what starrs they lived" (p. 381).

## IV. Summary.

Only the unusual importance of Daniel for this whole study can justify the amount of space that has been devoted to him. As was pointed out above, what his predecessors said on the historical point of view from 1570 to 1603 does not account in itself for the space given to them. We could not expect them to do more than assume a dogmatism drawn from classic sources, because the greater part of them had seen little of the national literature worth comparing, or even contrasting, with the classic literature from which the dogmatic rules were drawn. Elizabethan criticism arose from the two-fold attack of reformers, the attack of the Puritans and moralists on the base and scurrilous literature which tickled the ears of the groundlings before the great Elizabethan literature was born, and the attack of literary reformers whose patriotic zeal wished to give the English language and English poetry the perfection of the only great literature they knew. The first attack taking the form of the familiar medieval and renaissance citation of authorities, the defenders of poetry were compelled to crush their opponents by the citation of greater or more authorities, a wholly unhistorical procedure. The literary reformers were never wholly so dogmatic as to believe or assert that the English language or poetry could be treated exactly as Latin or Greek and their poetry; yet as a whole Elizabethan criticism spent itself largely in a dilettante fooling with exotic verse systems and a noble defense of poetry on moral and philosophical grounds.

In direct utterance on the historical point of view there are found in the whole period only a few odd sentences in Stanyhurst, King James, Nash and Harrington and one whole chapter in Puttenham which could have contributed to the statement of the historical point of view by Daniel. In the light of what had gone before and what followed for the next century and a half, Daniel's achievement was nothing less than remarkable. On the whole, no single essay is comparable to it before Hurd's *Letters on Chivalry and Romance* in 1762. Daniel not only gave the death blow to the craze for foreign meters, but he also re-established the credit of the Middle Ages. He affirmed a century before Du Bos that delight is the one test for poetry, and he showed finally that any successful poetry can only be composed in harmony with the spirit of its own age and its own national tradition and character. With this assertion of a relative standard of judgment he exhibited a tolerance wholly in keeping with such a breadth of view. With Daniel, then, Elizabethan criticism reached both its end and its climax.

---

# III. Seventeenth Century Criticism.[1]

## 1. General Division and General Characteristics.

The general divisions of seventeenth century criticism are more distinctly marked than those in the Elizabethan period. Gayley and Scott have two divisions for the seventeenth century, the first from Jonson to Cowley (Movement toward Practical Criticism), and the second from the founding of the Royal Society to the establishment of the *Tatler* (Refinement of Theory and Method).[2] In his *Literary Criticism in the Renaissance* Spingarn also makes a two-fold division, the first half of the century under Jonson's leadership toward "self-conscious art, guided by rules of criticism", and the second, the period of French influence, extending from 1651 to 1700.[3]

The last paragraph in Spingarn's *Introduction* to the *Critical Essays of the Seventeenth Century*, however, seems to negative to a degree what he said in 1899 and permitted to remain in the revision of his *Renaissance Criticism* in 1908, the date of the *Introduction* also. In the *Introduction* to the *Essays* he seems almost to have his earlier

[1] The references in this chapter to critical texts, unless otherwise noted, will be to Spingarn's *Critical Essays of the Seventeenth Century* and to Ker's *Essays of John Dryden.*

[2] *Lit. Crit.*, pp. 394—406.

[3] For his full division see pp. 254—260.

book in mind, when he says, "Literary history has inherited a traditional division of the seventeenth century into two arbitrary periods, each with a more or less definite and uniform outlook on literature; modern research and speculation have destroyed this very homogeneous impression. Seventeenth century criticism is really a very troubled stream, winds from every quarter blow across its surface; currents from many springs and tributaries struggle for mastery within it" (I. cv—cvi). A careful perusal of the three volumes of essays Spingarn has collected will tend to bring his reader to agree, in part, at least, with this last view. Yet it is possible to generalize enough to say that a division of the century into approximately equal halves corresponds to an actual change in the critical field; the first half saw the critical dominance of the last surviving Elizabethans, Bacon and Jonson, while the second half was marked by the introduction of the French critical influence.

In seventeenth century criticism as a whole one realizes a change in attitude and method which divides it from Elizabethan criticism. It is, in general, more intellectual and not so emotional or rhetorical in style. It is better organized, more scientific, if you will; it knows much more definitely what it is trying to do. The names of the first two seventeenth century critics are themselves significant of the change, merely in their relation to the general history of English literature. Bacon stands in English prose for the introduction of law and order into thought and style. He and Hooker are leaders in a new school of prose literature—grave, philosophical, methodical, as contrasting with the prose of Euphuism and Arcadian romance. Jonson in poetry is equally intellectual, equally methodical, as contrasted with contemporary romantic poets. It is only fitting that these men should stand in criticism at the threshold of a century in which the intellectual element was strong and the art of which was almost wholly self-conscious.

## 2. The First Half of the Seventeenth Century.

The first half of the seventeenth century opens with Bacon, includes Jonson and ends with Milton. The soberer, more weighty style, the more scientific, more intellectual and orderly handling of material, at least on the part of the dominant figures, Bacon and Jonson, sets the tone for the century.

Bacon's relation to the development of the historical point of view in literary study has already received some discussion. Gayley and Scott declare definitely, "Bacon is also the founder of literary history; he calls for the genetic method of critical study, by cause and effect, movement, influence, relation, change, decay and revival; and he suggests the elasticity of literary forms or types, ideas all essential to the understanding of literature as an historical growth".[1] Spingarn says practically the same thing (I. x). Flügel goes into the matter at greater length, and says categorically that Bacon did not have poetry—literature in our modern sense—in mind, when he gave his suggestions for a *History of Learning*.[2] Flügel's careful examination of the evidence is worthy of praise and we have to thank him for bringing together for comparison the significant passages of Bacon's own English version of the *Advancement of Learning* (1605) and the corresponding

---

[1] *Lit. Crit.*, p. 393. — [2] *Anglia*, XXI. 270.

Latin passages from *De Augmentis Scientiarum* (1623), with the English translation of the *De Augmentis* by Gilbert Wats (1740) printed in columns parallel with the Latin. Flügel bases his views on the meaning of *Literae* and *Artes* and *Scientiae* as used by Bacon.

After a careful reading of Bacon's contemporaries and predecessors in criticism and after a still more careful reading of the section in Book II of the *Advancement of Learning* and of Wats' almost contemporary translation of the corresponding sections of *De Augmentis*, I am unable to see how Professor Flügel can maintain his thesis. The best evidence against his views is contained in Bacon's own English in Book II of the *Advancement of Learning*. Bacon says: "The Parts of humane learning have reference to the three partes of Mans understanding, which is the seate of Learning: History to his Memory, Poesie to his Imagination, and Philosophie to his Reason" (I. 4). Here "Poesie" is one of the three parts of "humane learning." In the next paragraph Bacon goes on, "History is Natural, Civile, Ecclesiastical and Literary, whereof the three first I allow as extant, the fourth I note as deficient. For no man has propounded to himselfe the general, state of learning to bee described and represented from age to age, as many have done the works of Nature and the State civile and Ecclesiastical" (I. 4). Here he proposes a literary history, which is to describe from age to age the "generall state of learning." Is it likely he would use the word "learning" twelve lines above to include "poesie" and here use it to exclude "poesie", when the history is to be of the "generall state of learning?" The "particular sciences", the history of which has already been partly treated, are only parts of the whole—learning, and it is the "just story of learning" he is proposing (I. 5). Bacon begins his definition of "Poesie" further on by repeating, "Poesie is a part of Learning", and in the same paragraph calls it, "one of the principal Portions of Learning."[1]

Professor Flügel ought not to be able to get much comfort from Wats' literal translation of *De Augmentis.* It is true that in 1623 Bacon changed his divisions of history somewhat, from his arrangement in the *Advancement* of 1605, but the change does not effect the point at issue. Wats' translation of Chapter IV contains the following: "I. Civill History in our Judgement, is rightly divided into three Kindes; first into Sacred or Ecclesiastical; then into that which retaines the generall name Civill; lastly into that of Learning and Arts."[2] There is nothing here or later in the chapter to show that Bacon had changed his definition of "learning" since 1605 and we must assume that he meant by a "Just and Generall History of Learning"[3] a history of recorded human thought, of civilization if you will, but certainly of human achievement, whether in the arts, in science, in philosophy, or in "poesie."

Bacon's utterances on his "Literary History", then, are of prime importance for the purposes of this investigation. His criticism of the excessive study of style does not interest us, except when he shows a chain of causes which brought it about (I. 1—2). His definition of poetry as wholly the product of the imagination (I. 4 and 5) is of interest when we remember that the imagination had

---

[1] I. 5. Cf. Jonson's definition of "Poesy" as "Queene of Arts," I. 51, and Milton's inclusion of poetry among the "organic arts," I. 206.

[2] *Anglia,* XXI. pp. 263—264. — [3] *Ibid.,* 264.

almost to be rediscovered in the eighteenth century. The generating motive of poetry, as the desire to escape the real world (I. 6), is interesting for the same contrast it furnishes to the insistent realism of the neo-classicists. But his suggestions for the history of learning is of direct value to us. The passages in *De Augmentis* are fuller than those in the *Advancement of Learning* and therefore more interesting. Section II of Chapter IV begins as follows:

> "II. The *Argument is nothing else but a recitall from all Times, what Knowledges and Arts, in what Ages and Climates of the World have flourisht.* Let there be made a commemoration of their *Antiquities, Progresses* and *Perograttions*, through diverse parts of the world (for Sciences shift and move, as people do...) ... Let there be noted the *Chiefest Authors*, the *best Bookes*, *Schools*, *Successions*, *Universities*, Societies, Colledges, Orders, and Whatsoever else belongs to the State of Learning. But above all let this be observed (which is the Grace and Spirit of Civill History), that the Causes and Consultations be connexed with the events: namely that the *nature of Countries and People be recorded, the dispositions apt and able; or inept and inable for diverse disciplines: the Occurences of time Adverse, or Propitious to Learning, the Zeales and mixtures of Religions, the Discountenances, and favours of Lawes: and last, the eminent virtues and sway of Persons of note, for the promoting of Learning; and the like*".[1]

Then he advises as sources not merely histories and critiques but also a reading of the best books in the dif-

[1] *Anglia,* XXI. 264—266. The italics are Bacon's.

ferent periods, "that from a taste and observation of the argument, stile, and method thereof . . . the learned spirit of that age, as by a kind of charm, shall be awak't and rais'd up from the dead" (p. 266).

This is not a direct application of the historical, genetic method to literary criticism proper; indeed Bacon advises "that time be not wasted in praise and censure of particulars, after the manner of Critiques" (p. 266). But as a method to be applied to the study of literature, even in its history, it is of the highest significance for the further development of the historical point of view. Bacon insisted on an exposition of the causal relation between learning—of which literature is a part—and the forces that determine its development—racial, physical, religious, political and social. He understood that the unity of the human spirit did not permit the separation of its activities and products into air-tight compartments—"for the spirit of Man is the same, though the Revelation of Oracle and Sense be diverse".[1]

There is nothing especially new in Ben Jonson's criticism. In the *Prefaces* and other matter taken from his plays (1598—1601), printed in the *Appendix* to Gregory Smith's second volume, there is material that shows clearly the course Jonson is to take in his later critical work, for

---

[1] I. 4. It is to be noted that though the terminology of Bacon's psychology may be that of the "conventional Scholastic psychology," Bacon expressed at least one new psychological idea. In speaking of the effect of the drama as compared with other forms he says: "And certainly it is most true, and, as it were, a secret of nature, that the minds of men are more patent of affections and impressions Congregate than solitary"—(*De Augmentis,* quoted by Spingarn, I. 220)—certainly an early statement of "crowd psychology."

example, his exaltation of Poesie—"Attired in the maiestie of Arte", his appropriation of Whetstone's and Sidney's condemnation of irregular Drama, and his definition of "Humours".[1] That Jonson in 1599 had something of the Elizabethan independence can be seen in the speech of Cordatus: "I see not then but wee should enjoy the same *Licentia* or free power to illustrate and heighten our inuentions as they did; and not bee tied to those strict and regular forms which the niceness of a few (who are nothing but Forme) would thrust upon us." This direct slap at the use of a chorus, unity of time, etc., Jonson justifies in the same speech by showing that comedy grew from small beginnings, and "every man in the dignity of his spirit and iudgement" supplied something, that later men, like Plautus, "excluded *the Chorus*, altered the property of the persons, their names and natures, and augmented it with all libertie, according to the elegancie and disposition of those times wherein they wrote."[2] Three things should be noted in this speech of Cordatus—it is a real plea for liberty against arbitrary rules, but it is supported by an appeal to authority, and yet this appeal takes the form of a sketch of the development of comedy and ends with the notable clause—"and augmented it with all libertie according to the elegancie and disposition of those times wherein they wrote". This is practically Daniel's recognition of a standard of taste changing with the changing ages, but, like a classicist, Jonson supports his plea for liberty by appeal to classic example.

---

[1] Gregory Smith, II. 388, 389, 391.

[2] Smith, II. 393.

In the critical pieces by Jonson in Spingarn's first volume are the *Preface* to *Sejanus* (1605), *Dedication* to *Volpone* (1607), *Preface* to *The Alchemist* (1612) and the extracts from the *Discoveries* (1620—1635?). In the first he apologizes for departing from the rules with a rather sarcastic reference to the quality of his audience as the cause (I. 11). The *Discoveries*, as Spingarn points out, is little more than Jonson's commonplace book, made up of translations and occasional comments and additions of his own from Latin critics and from Heinsius and other continental critics (I. 221—222). He has a perfectly clear descent for Poesy, the "Queene of Arts, which had her Originall from heaven, received thence from the *Ebrewes*, and had in prime estimation with the *Greeks*, transmitted to the *Latines* and all Nations that profess'd Civility" (I. 51). His prescription for a poet (I. 52—54) is only an expansion of *Sidney's* Genius, Art, Imitation, Exercise.[1] "Aristotle was the first accurate Criticke and truest Judge" (I. 55), but it is ridiculous to make him a "*Dictator* when it is possible for us to make further discoveries of truth and fitnesse" (p. 43), and he does not believe it right "to conclude a Poets liberty within the narrow limits of lawes," for before these laws were made many excellent Poets fulfilled them.[2] All of which goes to show that Jonson was the founder in England of a reasonable, mild, but definite neo-classic system of conscious art, and therefore little was to be expected of him in the matter of genetic criticism.

Between Jonson and Milton the critics represented in Spingarn's first volume—including the citation in the

[1] G. Smith, I. 195. — [2] p. 56. Taken from Heinsius.

*Appendix* of the *Conversations* of Drummond and Jonson, Webster's *Preface* to the *White Devil* (1612), Chapman's *Prefaces* to his Homer (1610—1616?), Bolton's *Hypercritica* (1618?), Peacham's *Of Poetry* (1622), Drayton's *Epistle to Reynolds* (1627), Reynolds' *Mythomystes* (1633), Alexander's *Anacrisis* (1634) and Suckling's *Sessions of the Poets* (1637?) —are of but minor importance to us. Webster imitates Jonson's contempt for his audience, is tolerant of the different contemporary dramatic schools and wants his play to be read in the light of both Jonson and Shakespeare (p. 65—66). Chapman cites "Moses, David, Solomon, Job, Essay, Jeremy" as poets a century before Addison and insists again that Homer's work came from divine genius and not from conscious art.[1] He analyzes the special value of English as a poetic medium but, on the whole, adds little to his earlier prefaces.[2] Alexander declares for the "boundless Liberty of a Poet" and criticises the unhistorical interpretation of their models by the neo-classicists (I. 185). So far as we are concerned the others, with the exception of Bolton, may be wholly neglected.

Bolton's *Hypercritica, or a Rule of Judgment for Writing or Reading our History's*, is not so valuable in the field of literary criticism proper, but it is notable as the first serious attempt in English to consider the methods of historical study and composition. It antedates the next important English discussion of the subject, Bolingbroke's *Letters on the Study and Use of History*, by considerably over a century; yet some of the vital principles of histor-

---

[1] I. 67. Cf. *supra*, pp. 55—56.

[2] I. 77—79. Cf. Smith, II. 295—307.

ical method are found also in Bolton. He quotes Bodin and Bacon as leading authorities (I. 93 and 99). He regrets, as Bolingbroke did later, that there has been up to his time no "universal History for *England*" and his wish is "That the Majesty of Handling our History might once equal the Majesty of the Argument" (pp. 83 and 96). To this end he insists that "Indifferency and even dealing are the Glory of Historians", and he condemns the unhistorical reading into the "Narrations of things done fifteen or sixteen hundred years past" by historians of the "Jealousies, Passions, and Affections of their own Time" (pp. 91 and 93). Finally he insists that history must give the causal relation between events. He declares that "he who relates Events without their Premisses and Circumstances deserves not the name of an Historian," for here lies "the principle Difficulty and mystery of Historical Office, and not only Difficulty and Mystery, but Felicity also" (pp. 84 and 100). Bolton, then, has a distinct conception of the historian's office; but unfortunately he could not influence his contemporaries, since his book was not published until 1722. Its publication, then, is only another instance of the increased interest in history in the early eighteenth century, and the *Hypercritica* probably had its share of influence on Bolingbroke and the historians.

It is a commonplace to call Milton the last of the Elizabethans. The critical extracts from Milton given by Spingarn date from 1641 to 1671. Hardly ten years after the first date Davenant and Hobbes had initiated a new movement in criticism, and before the last date Cowley, Flecknoe, Dryden, Howard, Sprat and Shadwell had started Restoration criticism well on its way. There is nothing in Milton's critical work to show that he wrote in the middle of the seventeenth century rather than in the second half of the sixteenth except, perhaps, his absolute seriousness and his ever present feeling of dedication to a high and holy work. His dedication, he tells us in the *Reason of Church Government*, can be justified only by "labour and intent study . . . joyn'd with the strong propensity of nature",[1] which is no more than Jonson's and Sidney's prescription for the poet.[2] Like Ascham and his followers, he scorned the previous achievements of English verse "made small by the unskilfull handling of monks and mechanicks" (p. 196). In the *Treatise of Education* we find not only his famous contrast of Poetry with Rhetoric as "more simple, sensuous and passionate," but also the direction to learn this "sublime Art" in "*Aristotles poetics*, in *Horace* and the *Italian* commentaries of Castelvetro, Tasso, Mazzoni and others," who teach "what the laws are of a true *Epic* poem, what of a *Dramatic*, what of a *Lyric*, what decorum is, which is the grand masterpiece to observe" (p. 206). This is pure neo-classicism, of the Italian, and therefore Elizabethan variety, only six years before Davenant's introduction of French influences. Fourteen years later, in the *Preface* to *Paradise Lost*, Milton repeats the attack, now a hundred years old, against "Rime" as the "Invention of a barbarous Age," and considers that he has set the first example in English "of ancient liberty recover'd to Heroic Poem;" yet he does hedge a little with the phrase, "in longer works especially," and grants that rhyme has been graced by some famous modern poets, "carried away by Custom" (p. 207). Had

---

[1] I. 195; cf. 199. — [2] *Supra*, 74.

Milton not read Daniel's *Defence*? If he had, his sympathies, or prejudices, were too firmly fixed to be moved. The last bit of criticism from him, the *Preface* to *Samson Agonistes* in 1671, shows that his prejudices would let him see nothing good in the great Elizabethan tragedies (p. 208), and he boasts of following the Ancients and the Italians in the use of a Chorus, in handling the fable with verisimilitude and decorum and in observing the unity of time (p. 209). The instructional and moral office of poetry is always uppermost with Milton[1], he always writes to "justify the ways of God to man."

In three of the vital problems of criticism, then, the question of verse form, of dramatic form, and of the function of poetry, Milton, from our modern point of view, is on the wrong side. The statement of Gayley and Scott that Milton's "position in poetics, like that of Sidney and Bacon, is above strife"[2] certainly stands in need of qualification. Anyone must praise a few things in his criticism, especially the almost awful solemnity with which he regarded his high calling, the first preparation for which could come only by the help of that "eternal Spirit" who "sends out his Seraphim with the hallow'd fire of his Altar to touch and purify the lips of whom he pleases" (p. 199). He found good in the old romances (p. 203) and even considered whether, following the example of Tasso, he might not use "our own ancient stories" as (the subject of an epic, with the very significant proviso "that there be nothing advers in our climat or the fate of this age" (p. 196). Considerably more influential later, was his exaltation of the Bible as literature. *Job* is cited,

---

[1] Cf. 195, 197, 206. — [2] Work cited, p. 395.

with Homer, Virgil and Tasso, as a model for the epic. The *Song* of *Solomon* is a pastoral drama, *The Revelation* is the "majestick image of a high and stately Tragedy." The frequent songs throughout the Law and the Prophets "may be easily made appear over all the kinds of Lyrick poesy to be incomparable" (pp. 196—197). Here he expands upon Sidney and Chapman and prepares the way directly for the appreciation of biblical literature by Addison, Brown and others in the eighteenth century, an appreciation, in the opinion of Hamelius directly influential in the growth of the historical point of view.[1] But neither Milton's appreciation of the Bible as literature nor his one clause as to the influence of climate and the age on literary success can make of him anything more than an adherent of authority and the rules, and therefore never fundamentally capable of assuming the historical point of view in the consideration of literary questions.

## 3. The Second Half of the Century.

The first half of the century furnished only two writers of importance for the development of the historical point of view in criticism, but neither Bacon nor Bolton wrote extensively on criticism itself. Bacon introduced natural law, the force of historical environment in its various phases, as a necessary condition for the study of literary development. Bolton formulated the demands of good historical method in general. Jonson founded the neoclassic school in England. Milton belonged properly among the Elizabethan dogmatists.

The second half of the seventeenth century saw the formulation and fixing of the neo-classic creed. At the

[1] Work cited, 166; cf. 162—166.

same time, it expressed various phases of revolt, some times apologetic, sometimes open, against this creed. As was pointed out in the *Introduction*[1] and in connection with Jonson and Milton, the assumption of the dogmatic point of view, that is, adherence to the neo-classic creed, makes impossible a complete recognition of the historical point of view. Yet the rationalism of the second half of the century was necessarily in essence opposed to authority and any rules derived from authority; in deference to rationalism, when dogmatists like Rymer used the traditional rules they tried to justify them by "common sense". Moreover, rationalism and the new scientific movement were closely akin, and the latter proved favorable in such men as Cowley and Sprat toward tentative expressions of the genetic conception of literature. The school of taste in literature was allied with the natural science movement[2], and from this school of thought the chief rebels against authority came. It must be confessed that they are far from consistent in their rebellion.

It is not worth while here to point out in detail the rationalism of Davenant's *Preface* to *Gondibert* (1650) and the answer of Hobbes (1650) and his own *Preface* to *Homer* (1675). The Baconian imagination as a productive faculty becomes with them a matter of judgment, and fancy, which furnishes only the ornaments to poetry, must be controlled by reason.[3] Both have the charac-

---

[1] *Supra,* pp. 18 and 35—36.

[2] Spingarn I. xcff. Cf. for the various movements in the second half of the century Spingarn's excellent treatment in his *Introduction.* Yet Daniel certainly denied the right of a fixed standard in taste before Hobbes and Howard, whom Spingarn makes the originators of the revolt against authority in taste (p. xcvii).

[3] Cf. II. 11, 24—25, 58, 62, 63, 67, 70, 71.

teristic aristocratic tone of their party (pp. 14, 45, 55, 62). Davenant recognizes a difference in taste, considers the psychology of the reader and deliberately transgresses the rules (pp. 19—20). Hobbes sees that the invoking of the muse by heathen poets is explainable and excusable when we consider their religion (p. 58). But the whole conception of both men is rationalistic and they prepare the way for Rymer's "common sense".

In Cowley's *Preface* to his *Poems* (1656), we find something of the scientific attitude toward literature, as might be expected from one of the leaders in the new scientific movement. In his paragraph on the relative influences of peace and war he also refers to climatic influence—"if *wit* be such a *Plant* that it scarce receives heat enough to preserve it alive even in the *Summer* of our cold *Clymate*, how can it choose but wither in a long and sharp *winter*?—a warlike, various and tragical age is best to *write of*, but worst to write in." He carries this directly over to the influence of outward circumstances upon the mood of the artist and combines the historical and the psychological points of view when he says of Ovid that "The *cold* of the Countrey had strucken through all his faculties, and benummed the very *feet* of his *verses*" (II. 80—81). He, too, understands that the "mad stories of the *Gods* and *Heroes*" in ancient poetry grew out of "the *Theologie* of those times", and then he proceeds to praise the Bible as literature even more extravagantly than his predecessors (pp. 89—90). If we had his proposed "Discourse concerning Style," according to Sprat's account of it (p. 142), we should certainly have a further application of the historical point of view.

Flecknoe's *Short Discourse of the English Stage* (1664),

Shadwell's two *Prefaces* (1668—1671), Phillips's *Preface* to the *Theatrum Poetarum* (1675), Glanvill's *Concerning Preaching* (1678), Rochester's *Allusion to Horace* (1677—79?), Mulgrave's *Essay upon Poetry* (1682), Roscommon's *Essay on Translated Verse* (1684) and the letters of Evelyn in the *Appendix* to Volume II need not detain us. Flecknoe's sketch of stage history is not in the least genetic. Shadwell glories in obeying the rules. Phillips is really conservative, opposes "romantic" actions, but throws the rules overboard in favor of Spenser and Shakespeare. Glanvill is out of our field. The three noble lords write well for lords, but they are wholly pseudo-classic. There remains for discussion in Spingarn's second volume, then, Howard, Spratt, the great representative of Good Sense, Rymer, and the man who satirized him, Butler.

Howard's first *Preface* (to *Four New Plays,* 1665) makes some attempt to justify the English drama against a slavish following of classic or French models, because "the manner of the Stage-Entertainments have differ'd in all Ages", but he is against tragi-comedy (pp. 98—100). In his attack on rhyme he attempts an argument on the psychology of dramatic illusion (pp. 101—102). His *Preface* to *The Duke of Lerma* (1668) is an answer to Dryden's *Essay of dramatic Poesie.* In this *Preface* we find the first complete assertion since Daniel that taste is the final arbiter and not external rules. "I confess", he says, "'tis not necessary for poets to study strict reason", and just before he had declared the whole matter: "Nor do I condemn in the least any thing of what Nature soever that pleases, . . . I rather blame the unnecessary understanding of some that have labour'd to give strict rules to things that are not Mathematical; . . . for in the difference of *Tragedy* and *Comedy*, and of *Fars* it self, there can be no determination but by the Taste; nor in the manner of their Composure"; (pp. 106—107). This is inconsistent, delightfully and necessarily so, with what he said three years before on tragi-comedy. Here, however, he would have "all attempts of this nature be submitted to the fancy of others" and then he will "not discommend any Poet that dresses his Play in such a fashion as his fancy best approves" (p. 110).

Sprat's *History of the Royal Society* (1667) and his *Life of Cowley* (1668) show a little of Howard's inconsistency. In the former Sprat is discussing style. He pleads for the founding of an English Academy with absolute authority in questions of style, and criticism generally, "a fixt and *Impartial Court of Eloquence*, according to whose Censure all Books or Authors should either stand or fall"—a favorite proposal from others also,[1] but doomed because of the character of the English[2] never to be realized. His *Criticisms of Cowley* are conservative, almost naive. He praises the variety of measure in Cowley's odes chiefly because of "its near affinity with Prose" (p. 132). Yet he thinks that the reasons why oratory differs in France and England is because of the difference in the manner of life (p. 112). He prophesies an outburst of good historical writing in England from a historical parallel between it and Rome. Then he confidently expects to realize the great stylistic ideal of the Royal Society — "so many *things* almost in an equal number of *words*"—because of "the general constitution of the minds of the *English*." He concludes with a positive statement of the influence

[1] Cf. Note, II. 337—8. — [2] Cf. Temple, III. 10 —107.

of both race and environment—"the position of our climate, the air, the influence of heaven, the composition of the English blood, as well as the embraces of the ocean" (pp. 118—119).

We cannot accuse Rymer of being inconsistent or of not realizing fully what he was about. His second sentence in his *Preface* to his translation of Rapin (1674) is the statement in essence of his whole point of view—"Poets would grow negligent, if the Criticks had not a strict eye over their miscarriages" (p. 162)—a complete statement of the "judicial"—dogmatic attitude. "Good Sense" is his slogan, and the authority of Aristotle would not be respected, "were not the reasons convincing and clear as any demonstration in Mathematicks" (p. 165). Only reasonable, probable poetry has any life in it (p. 171). The only people who have the audacity not to observe the rules of Aristotle are the Arabs, and it is to their wild, vast and unbridled fancy that we owe the introduction of "Riming" into Europe, he "supposes" (p. 165). In the *Tragedies of the Past Age considered and examin'd by the Practice of the Ancients and by the Common Sense of all Ages* (1678), the title is sufficient indication that he continues in the way of his first *Preface*. In fact, he goes much further. He understands exactly where the chief attacks on his system come from, so he states them and tries to meet them before they are urged. He takes them in order. First there is the objection of the school of taste, which Howard has already urged, but Rymer calls those who make "what will *please*" their standard "*Stage-quacks* and *Empericks* in Poetry" (p. 183). Then he states the objection of those who take the historical point of view—"There is also another great *accident* [Wotton used the word in exactly this connection sixteen years later (III. 208)], which is that *Athens* and *London* have not the same *Meridian*"—and he answers, "Certain it is that *Nature* is the same, and *Man* is the same" (II. 184). Then in answer to the objection of the claims of the imagination—"Poetry is the *Child* of *Fancy*, and is never to be school'd and *disciplin'd* by *Reason*"—he restates the doctrine of the necessary control of Fancy by Reason, already stated by Davenant and Hobbes[1], and calls those "*Fanaticks* in Poetry" who urge inspiration, enthusiasm, "*rapture* and *rage* all over" (II. 185). It would have been interesting to have had a Homeric encounter on the point between Rymer and Chapman. That rules would restrain the creative imagination and present a pleasing variety in invention he answers by saying that "*Nature* affords plenty and variety enough of *Beauties*" (II. 185).—"Nature" is an extremely handy word for the neo-classicist![2]—Rymer knew, then, just what his system involved and he himself has formulated the objections of its enemies that were bound finally to destroy it. That with such principles he should condemn Chaucer, Spenser, Milton and Shakespeare[3] follows as a matter of course. Moreover he says that the rudeness of the "Poetry of the last age" is due to the fact that the great poets did not study Aristotle and Homer enough.[4] Rymer is far from being the worst critic that ever lived, but his principles are the apotheosis of that dogmatic criticism with which the historical point of view must necessarily come into conflict, and he is at

---

[1] Cf. *Supra*, p. 80.

[2] Cf. I. lxvii—lxviii.

[3] II. 167, 208, and the whole *Short View*.

[4] 207. Cf. Ch. VII, in the *Short View* of 1693 (pp. 219—255).

least to be praised for calling out protests against his principles.

Certainly the most enjoyable of these protests is Butler's *Upon Critics Who Judge of Modern Plays Precisely by the Rules of the Antients* (1678?). Butler's verse attack makes use chiefly of wit and ridicule, but it is none the less clever and shrewd. It is a pity not to be able to quote it entire. He opens with the question:

"Who ever wil Regard Poetique Fury,
When it is once found Idiot by a Jury?"

Rymer's attempt is to

"Reduce all Tragedy by Rules of Art,
Back to its Antique Theater, a Cart."

And even a Puppet Play must be so ruled,

"That not an Actor shal Presume to Squeek
Unless he hav a Licence for't in Greek,
Nor Whittington Henceforward sel his Cat in
Plaine vulgar English, without Mewing Latin."

Further

"An English Poet should be tryd b'his Peres
And not by Pedants & Philosophers,
Incompetent to Judge Poetique Fury,
As Butchers are forbid to b'of a Jury;
Beside the most Intollerable wrong,
To try their matters in a Forrain Tongue."

Here Butler speaks for the "wits" and declares that Rymer is merely a filcher from "virtuosi-Tuscans" and others (II. pp 278—280).

It may be as well to get rid at once of those men in Volume III of Spingarn's collection who have little or no significance for this study. Wolseley's *Preface to Rochester's Valentinian* (1685) is merely a defence of Rochester against the attack of the moralists, on the principle that not matter but manner counts. The whole thing is neo-classic even to that epigrammatic statement, "every Ass that's Romantick believes he's inspired".[1] Langbaine's essay on Dryden in his *English Dramatic Poets* (1691), is simply detailed proof of Dryden's plagiarizing. Gildon's *Vindication of Paradise Lost* (1694) is, even as an attempt, of general interest, and one idea has perhaps some special interest for us, that is, that Milton's blindness was one cause of his success (III. 200). Blackmore's *Preface to Prince Arthur* (1695) praises the "incomparable rules" and "great models" and acknowledges as his masters Aristotle, Horace, Rapin, Dacier, Bossu and "our own *excellent Critick* Mr. Rymer" (p. 240). Collier's famous *Short View* (1698) shows him to be not merely a moral reformer but also a shrewd critic, after the manner of Rymer. Lansdowne's *Upon unnatural Flights in Poetry* (1701) shows him to be what the word "Unnatural" suggests, a mere follower of the School of Sense.

This leaves us free to take up the more important men left before 1700,—Temple, Dennis, Wotton, Congreve and Dryden. All of these men wrote in the last decade of the century, but Dryden, of course, had begun to write a quarter of a century before. Here, though in some cases the material grows larger, the treatment will have to be briefer. So far it has been possible to quote very largely all that has been said bearing on the subject of the investigation, and it seemed desirable to do so because we were still, in a degree, dealing with beginnings. It still seemed necessary, also, to make clear exactly what critical views were opposed to the historical point of view.[2]

---

[1] III. 12. Cf. Phillip's use of the word "romantic", II. 268.

[2] Cf. *supra*, p. 44.

But from now on it will be necessary to use considerable compression, a compression, however, that will still enable the reader to find his way through the as yet untouched eighteenth century path of the historical point of view.

After Daniel, we must give the credit to Sir William Temple for making the next largest use of the historical method before 1700, and Temple added elements that Daniel lacked. Temple's essays on the *Ancient and Modern Learning*, *Poetry*, *and Heroick Virtue* (1690) all contain something bearing on the subject. He went into the quarrel between the Ancients and the Moderns nominally on the side of the ancients. He is really, however, to be numbered among the *Virtuosi*, a member of the school of Taste, and therefore can justify the Ancients and still like the Moderns. He is one of the first Englishmen to become interested in the early Scandinavian literature. In connection with what he calls the "Sonnet" of Regner Lodbrag, he not only says it is well worth reading, "by any that love Poetry," but he also asks his readers "to consider the several stamps of that Coyn, according to several ages and climates."[1] In the essay on *Ancient and Modern Learning* he suggests Young's whole argument on original genius and by implication upsets the "Wanted Art" argument against Shakespeare, for, he points out, learning may actually tend to suppress genius, and he asks the significant question: "May there not many circumstances concur to one production that do not to any other in one or many ages?"[2] The essay on *Poetry* is, in spite of some drawbacks, surprisingly modern, not in

[1] Cited by Farley, *Scandinavian Influences*, p. 64.

[2] III. 46—48; cf. p. 80.

the sense of the Quarrel. He asserts that genius is the "pure and free Gift of Heaven or of Nature," and this genius is "too libertine to be confined to so many Rules" (pp. 80, 84). He is still much interested in Runic poetry; he believes that late Latin poetry and the medieval Latin rhymesters learned their verse forms by "Gothic imitation" (pp. 79—80, 92—94). The new medieval poetry of necessity had to be different from classic poetry, because it was the result of a "New Face of Customs, Habit, Language, and almost Nature" (p. 98).

Then comes the long passage (pp. 103—107) in which he asserts that the English drama is the best of all, ancient or modern, because of the vein of humor natural to the English. The reason why humor is superior to comedy in general is that "Humour is but a Picture of particular Life, as Comedy is of general; and that it represents Dispositions and customs less common, yet they are not less natural than those that are more frequent among men".[1] Here Temple casts another bombshell into the neo-classic camp. This is the assertion of the romantic principle that the individual, the exceptional, may be just as true and is certainly more interesting than the generalized types of neo-classicism.

The next three pages contain a perfectly definite statement of the chain of causes which has produced the greater variety and individuality in English life out of which grows the greater attractiveness of the English drama. This attractive individuality comes from "the Native plenty of our soil, the unequalness of our Clymat, as well as the Ease of our government." "Plenty," he says, "begets

---

[1] p. 103; cf. p. 104.

Wantonness and Pride: Wantonness is apt to invent, and pride scorns to imitate. Liberty begets Stomach or Heart, and Stomach will not be Constrained. Thus we come to have more Originals, and more that appear what they are; we have more Humour, because every man follows his own, and takes a Pleasure, perhaps a Pride, to shew it" (p. 104). He points out that a sameness in life must result from opposite conditions and then proceeds to show that the changeable climate is responsible for the fact that, "we are not only more unlike one another than any Nation I know, but we are more unlike ourselves too at several times" (p. 105). The result of all this may be bad in some ways, but it has at least made the English drama excel all others through its humor.

Temple's contribution is, then, most significant. He exalts original genius above the conscious rules of dogmatic art, whether Jonson's or Rymer's. He sees the indebtedness of the medieval poetry of culture to the despised northern tongues. This with his sympathetic appreciation of Scandinavian poetry places him with Daniel and Hurd and the Wartons as a prophet of the coming romanticism. Finally he accounts for a great literary achievement by specific reference to national character and for this to national environment.

Any student of English criticism must regret that we have no collection of John Dennis' critical essays. One who works at any other place than the British Museum will probably have to miss most of them. Only two of his essays as wholes, out of a dozen or more that one ought to read for a comprehensive view of his criticism, are easily accessible, *The Impartial Critick* of 1693 and *On the Genius and Writings of Shakespeare* of 1711; but these are the most important for our purposes. *A Large Account of Taste in Poetry* (1702) shows that the reason for the superior taste in comedy under Charles II as compared with the condition in 1702 was a change in the general tendency of the times, and *The Grounds of Criticism in Poetry* (1704) cites and praises masses of poetry in the Bible. That is all for us except what is found in the two typical essays first mentioned. Saintsbury rightly gives rather unusual space to Dennis, and there a reader can get a general view of his work.[1] The *Impartial Critick* was called out directly by Rymer's *Short View.* Unlike Temple, Dennis did not belong to the school of taste. He was often individual in his views, but was intermittently a stickler for the rules, and in general an adherent of the school of sense. In the *Impartial Critick,* for example, "Freeman," the mouthpiece of Dennis himself, says, "The Rules of *Aristotle* are nothing but Nature and Good Sense reduced to a Method"[2], which is only Rymer's formula before him and Pope's after him. In this essay, however, he sets up the historical standard which Rymer foresaw as an enemy to his system. The second sentence begins: "For to set up the Grecian Method amongst us with success, it is absolutely necessary to restore not only their Religion and their Polity, but to transport us to the same Climate in which *Sophocles* and *Euripides* writ" (p. 148). The difference in the treatment of love in classic Athens and in England is due to "difference of Climate and Customs" (p. 150—151). The difference between Waller and Voiture is due to the difference in the character of the two nations (p. 153). Nevertheless Dennis judges

---

[1] *Hist. of Crit.,* II. 431—437. — [2] Spingarn, III. 194.

Dryden's *Oedipus* by Aristotle's rules (p. 166 ff.). The essay on Shakespeare[1] takes the conventional late seventeenth and early eighteenth century patriotic English view of Shakespeare. The dramatist is one of the greatest geniuses the world ever saw, his beauties wholly the result of his own genius, his faults due to his education and age.[2] Yet "If Shakespeare had these great Qualities by Nature, what would he not have been, if he had joined to so happy a Genius Learning and the Poetical Art?"[3] Those who claim that Shakespeare "had Learning and a familiar Acquaintance with the Ancients" really detract from his extraordinary merit and the "Glory of Great Britain", for the country may justly claim a great share in the nature and genius of such an unlearned phenomenon as Shakespeare, "since these depend in a great measure on the Climate." In other words, eighteen years after the *Impartial Critick* Dennis still believes, then, at the same time in the efficacy of the Rules and in the influence of environment on the production of genius. He remains a dogmatist with occasional flashes of insight into principles wholly inconsistent with his dogmatism.[4]

Wotton's *Reflections upon Ancient and Modern Learning* (1694) is a reply to Temple's essay of 1690. In general, Wotton's tone is philosophical, temperate and unprejudiced. There is no doubt but that he was directly influential on Du Bos and Brown, men who took the

---

[1] D. Nichol Smith, *Eighteenth Century Essays on Shakespeare*, 24—46.

[2] *Ibid*, 24. — [3] *Ibid*, 26.

[4] Paul's *John Dennis: His Life and Criticism* reached me too late for citation above. Paul gives for the first time a study of Dennis commensurate with his importance. Cf. for the material above, pp. 153—155.

historical point of view at the end of the first and second quarters of the eighteenth century, yet his use of the genetic method is neither so great nor so clearly marked as Temple's. Wotton is entirely fair to the Ancients. He concedes a good deal when he says that the best modern writers of either prose or poetry have been "those who have read the Ancients with greatest care and endeavoured to imitate them with the greatest accuracy" (III. 203). This is as definite a statement of the principle of conscious imitative art as Rymer or Dennis would have made. But if the Ancients are superior, he asks, "What can be the reasons of this Disparity?" There are several reasons, reasons that quite take away a blind admiration for the classics and make our estimate more useful because less superstitious. One of these reasons is the superior character of the Greek language as an instrument of poetry (p. 204). A second reason for the superiority of Grecian eloquence is that the Grecian states were democracies, and democracies of long continuance because of their physical conditions, and therefore eloquence was a necessity (pp. 207—208). Latin poetry could not equal Greek poetry because Latin was not so ductile. Its majestic gravity, which came from the nature of the Romans, made it suitable for philosophical and epic poetry, but the Romans lacked the sprightliness of temper and the gaiety of the Greeks and their language did not have the variety of feet found in Greek, hence in some kinds of poetry they could not equal the Greeks (p. 209). Roman eloquence was fostered by the same conditions as in Greece, but it fell with Roman liberty. "It is Liberty alone", Wotton says, "which inspires Men with Lofty Thoughts and elevates their Souls to a higher Pitch than Rules of Art can direct" (p. 211). The Ancients surpassed the moderns in eloquence, but with the same concurrent circumstances we too might have a Demosthenes or a Cicero (p. 213). In history we may surpass them if we live up to a histor ical ideal which includes passing judgment upon "the Conduct of every People from the several Constitutions of their respective Governments, or from the Characters and Circumstances of the Actors themselves." In other words, Wotton believes that the result of a proper historical point of view ought to be a wise tolerance in judgment.

Congreve's letter to Dennis *Concerning Humour in Comedy* (1695), repeats what had now become an article of faith with several Englishmen, that the English were superior to the rest of the world in comedy. Congreve can only follow Temple in attributing this superiority to the quality of the English humour, and the humour itself he attributes to the same causes, "the greater Freedom, Privilege, and Liberty which the Common People of *England* enjoy" (III. 252), and to their feeding on flesh, but that, too, is only another aspect of Temple's "Native Plenty". In *A Discourse on the Pindaric Ode* (1706 or 1710?), however, Congreve really shows himself an adherent of regularity. He wishes English poets to follow Pindar in the regular construction of odes and attacks the irregularity of Cowley's followers. Congreve, then, is only significant by lending his authority to the principles of Temple.

Dryden has been left for discussion until the end of this chapter, but not because he is more important for the development of the historical point of view. He has been reserved for the last because his work stretches over the larger part of the second half of the century and because of his general critical importance. As a matter of fact, his utterances on the question we are discussing are comparatively slight in value. This study has already made plain, I hope, that there is an inevitable conflict between the dogmatic position in criticism and the historical standpoint. Dryden is sometimes called the father of English criticism. He has been given this title in recent times not because of the masses of dogmatic criticism found throughout his work, but because of occasional passages of unusually happy appreciative criticism, especially of Shakespeare and Chaucer.

Dryden's work as a critic was itself an excellent example of the influence of environment. He began to write before the neo-classic creed had been completely stated. He watched its growth, tried to conform to it occasionally in his original work, or suffered from the critics for not conforming to it, and he lived long enough to see the first open and weighty attacks upon it. His own temperament was really marked by a catholic openness to the appeal of various kinds, styles and periods in literature. This appreciation, however, was limited by his own chief interests as a producer of original literature, that is, his native interest in style, in expression, for its own sake, and in the life of man, in human character. He did not have the necessary historical outlook and standpoint to appreciate Chaucer's style, but he appreciates as fully as any man who has written since, Chaucer's remarkable achievement in creating character. He was a man quickly responsive to the thought and feeling of his own time and naturally paid especial attention to its theories about his own art and about the author he loved. The result is that his criticism reflects all the currents and cross-currents of his time.[1] It is all either occasional, a preface or a pedication prefixed to the particular piece of original work he is just publishing, or else it is more or less hack-work. Much of it lacks originality; he often merely transcribes the learning of others. It becomes original only when he revolts against the orthodox canon when it stands in the way of his own performance, or when his appreciation for his great predecessors must find vent. I doubt if it can be proved that Dryden was wholly consistent on any one of the vexed questions of criticism.[2] Sometimes he bowed to the critical yoke, sometimes he pulled away from it apologetically for awhile, and sometimes he openly revolted.

Bohn points out in his study of *The Development of John Dryden's Literary Criticism*[3] that Dryden's tendencies toward conformity or revolt were influenced also by his external relations to the court and to the prevailing social forces at any particular time. From 1666 to 1675, for example, Dryden is writing heroic plays, is more or less in favor at court and therefore open to pseudo-classic rational influences. From 1675 to 1679 he is out of favor, he writes to please himself and is in revolt against pseudo-classic standards. From 1680 to 1689 he is the literary defender of James II; he writes little criticism and what he does is orthodox. From 1690 to 1700 he is out of favor again at court and appeals directly for support to the reading public, and here his critical independence

---

[1] Cf. Spingarn, *Crit. Essays*, I. cvi.

[2] Ker asserts that he is. Cf. *Essays of John Dryden*, I. xxiii.

[3] *Pubs. Mod. Lang. Assoc.* XXII. 56—139. This is one of the most recent (1907) and one of the best of the numerous studies on Dryden's criticism.

comes back again and he reaches his best appreciative work in the *Preface to the Fables* in 1700.[1] With some striking inconsistencies in different periods, this corresponds, it seems to me, to the facts in the development of Dryden's criticism. Remembering, then, that Dryden is enthusiastic over the particular point of view he assumes at any particular time, and that he is forced constantly to compromise between his respect for authority, and the necessity "to please" in his own work and to justify his love for the national literary heroes, we can pass on to a discussion, brief as compared to the total amount of his criticism and its general value, of his relation to the historical point of view.

Dryden's first criticism, the *Dedication* to *The Rival Ladies* (1664), is significant. The play is a tragi-comedy, he wishes for an authoritative academy, and he praises rhyme, because it aids the judgment to curb the fancy. This gave rise to Howard's first preface against rhyme (1665). Then in the *Preface* to *Annus Mirabilis* (1667) he laments the "slavery of rhyme," but justifies his use of Davenant's stanza (I. 12). Such a rapid about-face is typical of his changes in point of view. The next essay, *Of Dramatic Poesy* (1668), is one of his most important critical pieces. It was occasioned by Howard's attack on rhyme. In general Dryden (Neander) defends rhyme against blank verse and the English against the French. Here we find a few expressions tending toward the genetic conception. "Every Age," he says, "has a kind of universal genius, which inclines those that live in it to some particular studies." Crites (Howard) says that an ancient

[1] Bohn, article cited, *passim.*

poet wrote of love as it was then the custom to make it and would have accommodated himself to our age if he lived now. Lisideius (Sedley) says, with Cowley, that the Muses follow peace. In his defence of the English against the French Dryden points out the evil results of the servile observation of the unities by the French and says Shakespeare was "naturally learned". In his defense of rhyme he quotes Daniel and abuses his argument of "universal consent." Finally, he asserts the doctrine of progress and therefore the poets of his own age are better rhymers than the Elizabethans, for "the genius of every age is different."[1] In his *Defence* of the *Essay* (1668) against Howard's assertion of a varying standard according to taste[2] Dryden defends the rules (I. 125 ff.).

The prefaces and dedications from 1668 to 1678 are in the main flattery of his patrons, or merely affirm his orthodoxy. But in 1678 came three expressions much more liberal, because, perhaps, he could write to please himself, since he was out of favor, and, moreover, Rymer had gone too far in his savage attack on the English poets Dryden loved.[3] In the *Preface* to *Oedipus* he says he and his collaborator, Lee, have followed the admirable Sophocles, as closely as they could, but the Athenian theatre (whether more perfect than ours, is not now the question) "had a perfection differing from ours."[4] In the *Preface* to *All for Love* he sneers at French correctness, and declares, "But for my own part, I desire to be tried by the laws of my own country;"[5] he praises Rymer's judicious observations that the Ancients ought to be our

[1] I. 36, 55, 56, 76, 80, 97—98, 99. — [2] Cf. *Supra*, pp. 82—83.
[3] Cf. *Supra*, p. 84 ff. — [4] *Works*, VI. 133.
[5] *Essays*, I. 194—195.

masters, "Yet, though their models are regular, they are too little for English tragedy;" and he professes to imitate the style of the "divine Shakespeare" (p. 200). Still more significant are the *Heads* of an *Answer* to *Rymer* (1678?). Here comes the famous sentence: "'Tis not enough that Aristotle has said so, for Aristotle drew his models of tragedy from Sophocles and Euripides; and, if he had seen ours, he might have changed his mind."[1] Here, too, he asserts that Shakespeare and Fletcher pleased because they wrote "to the genius of the age and nation in which they lived," and "the climate, the age, the disposition of the people to whom a poet writes, may be so different, that what pleased the Greeks would not satisfy an English audience" (XV. 385). Unfortunately, Dryden did not publish this before his death.

The very next year in the *Grounds* of *Criticism* in *Tragedy* Dryden practically accepts Rymer's whole position[2] and again there is a dearth of material until we reach the *Preface* to Don Sebastian (1690) when, though he accepts Rymer's doctrine of poetic justice, yet he merely kept the three mechanic rules of unity "in his eye" and "followed them at a distance." since the genius of the English will not tolerate a regular play.[3] The *Dedication* of the *Examen Poeticum* (1693) was partly occasioned by Rymer's *Short View*, and he declaims against "those who manifestly aim at the destruction of our poetic church and state," i. e., Rymer, and declares that many Elizabethan tragedies were "without comparison" beyond those of the Greeks and that the differences between the English and the French dramas

---

[1] *Works,* XV. 390. — [2] *Essays,* I. 211.

[3] *Works,* VII. 312.

are due to the difference in taste of the two peoples.[1] In a letter to Dennis (1693—94) he asserts that the English are ahead not only in comedy but also in tragedy "in spite of Mr. Rymer," for which Shakespeare had a genius and genius alone is greater virtue "than all other qualifications put together."[2] After that in the *Dedication of Love Triumphant* he practically repeats the chief head of his *Answer to Rymer*, that had Aristotle seen the *Cinna* of Corneille "I am confident he would have altered his opinion."[3] And that is all.

## 4. Summary.

Important, then, as Dryden is for criticism in general in the last half of the century, in our special field he is less important than others. In the seventeenth century as a whole, the great literary figures along with Dryden are Jonson and Milton, while in criticism Jonson, Rymer and Dryden are dominant figures. They were all men of power, and, with the exception of Dryden's occasional revolts, they used their power in support of dogmatism. Milton's dogmatism was unreasoned; Jonson's neo-classicism preached with force the doctrine of conscious art and judicious imitation of the classics; Rymer's dogmatism was based on what he claimed to be, and what generally was, a consistent rationalism.

For us, however, the important men in the century are not these dominant figures, but Bacon and Temple, and, in a lesser degree, Bolton, Cowley, Howard, Sprat, Butler, Dennis, Wotton, Congreve and occasionally Dryden himself. Bacon proposed that general method and point

---

[1] *Essays,* II. 5—7. — [2] *Works,* XVIII. 117. — [3] *Ibid.,* VIII. 247.

of approach in literary study which had to wait for its full realization till the nineteenth century, but his influence showed at once on Bolton, later in the century in the impetus toward scientific study, and in the beginning of the eighteenth century on Vico and Bolingbroke. Temple exalted original genius over rules, enjoyed the new northern poetry, and applied the historical method with considerable fullness and success in explaining one important literary phenomenon. The other men helped, positively or negatively, to promulgate the new method. Finally Rymer, the great representative of dogmatism, recognized the historical point of view openly as one of the chief foes of his system.

---

# IV. Eighteenth Century Criticism before 1770.

## 1. Grouping of the Critics.

Investigators of eighteenth century criticism find themselves severely handicapped by the fact that for that century no such convenient collections of all the critical material exist as those of Gregory Smith and Spingarn for the sixteenth and seventeenth centuries. Only one book assembles any number of the essays of the eighteenth century and those are all on one subject,—*Eighteenth Century Essays on Shakespeare*, edited by D. Nichol Smith. For the rest the student must do the best he can. The essays of the better known men are easily found, but many of the others are hard to get at. A few I have been unable to find in the libraries accessible to me; but none among those few is of any special importance for this study, so far as I have been able to determine from Saintsbury's *History* and other sources. Fortunately a number of the critical works of this period need no consideration here. Purely technical essays on the "art" of poetry and those dealing with the new field of aesthetics can, in the main, be frankly neglected. Among these are such works as Bysshe's *Art of Poetry* (1700), Gildon's *Complete Art of Poetry* (1718), Hutchinson's *Inquiry into the Original of our Ideas of Beauty and Virtue* (1725),

Harris' *Hermes* (1750), Hogarth's *Analysis of Beauty* (1753), Burke's *The Sublime and Beautiful* (1756), Kames' *Elements of Criticism* (1761), and D. Webb's *Remarks on the Beauty of Poetry* (1762). The other critics, contrary to my practice in the times of beginnings in the last two chapters, I shall notice only in so far as they have a fairly close relation to the development of the historical point of view.

It is not advisable to follow a strictly chronological order in discussing the critics between 1700 and 1770; some little grouping in accordance with subject matter and critical outlook will make the progress of critical thought somewhat clearer. Saintsbury has followed this principle rather than mere chronology in his treatment of the eighteenth century critics. In his first chapter of Book VI, Volume II, under the head of "Eighteenth Century Orthodoxy" he treats various critics from Addison to Johnson. In the next volume and next book under the general head of "The Dissolvents of Neo-Classicism" he gives Chapter III to "The English Precursors", and includes the various critics with romantic tendencies before Wordsworth. I have already pointed out the connection between romanticism and the growth of the historical point of view.[1] The recognition of the principles of romanticism in early eighteenth century criticism was likely to be associated with a more or less clear assumption of the historical conception of literature, though not always. In the main, the works of greatest interest to us come after 1750 while after that time there are not many—Johnson is the most conspicuous example—who are generally orthodox. In accordance with the principle just stated, I shall group

---

[1] *Supra*, pp. 4 and 15—16.

the various essays and prefaces on Shakespeare together. Since the bulk of these come before 1750, this will enable me to discuss Johnson's work along with that of the men with whom he sympathized more than with those who were writing when he wrote his *Preface* to *Shakespeare* in 1765.

## 2. Before 1725.

The critics writing before Pope's *Preface to Shakespeare* in 1725 who call for discussion here are chiefly Shaftesbury, Steele and Addison. Rowe will be noticed with the Shakespearean essays. Before Shaftesbury, however, one significant voice was raised in direct opposition to the rules. In Farquhar's *Miscellanies* (1702) appeared an *Essay on Comedy,* in which the dramatist says boldly, "The rules of English comedy don't lie in the compass of Aristotle or of his followers." In principles of law we do not go to the archives of Greece and Rome; hence the same rule should hold in poetry and we should get our learning and rules from our own playwrights. "But it must be so", he satirizes, "because Aristotle said it! Now I say it must be otherwise, because Shakespeare said it." Shakespeare was not only the greater poet, but because he was the better poet, "he must have the most judgment in his art."[1] This definite assertion that each great poet can best make his own rules and that each nation is a law unto itself is much more in the spirit of Daniel than in that of the eighteenth century Shakespearean critics, as we shall see. But Farquhar in 1702 was a voice crying

---

[1] *The Dramatic Works of Wycherly, Congreve, Vanbrugh and Farquhar,* pp. lx—lxi.

in the wilderness, a prophet certainly unheeded in his own country.

It is easy to overrate the value of Shaftesbury to literary criticism. What influence he had in criticism was chiefly in the field of aesthetics, where Saintsbury rightly discusses him.[1] Nevertheless in the midst of his discussions of the beautiful and the good in the *Characteristics* (1711) there are some passages to show his critical outlook. These prove that Shaftesbury was a pseudo-classicist. The British muses still lisp in their cradles even after the "rules of writing" have been stated. The only justification for the infantile state of Shakespeare and Milton, their rudeness and rawness, is that they wrote blank verse and were moral. England got all her civilization elsewhere. There is a fixed standard in nature somewhere for virtue and beauty and hence the need of critics against those who make "their humour alone the rule of what is beautiful and agreeable".[2] But he does restate Wotton's ideas that freedom is necessary to the development of tragedy and eloquence, and that the reason why Greece founded and perfected all the arts and at last, "even critics themselves acknowledged and received as masters over all the rest," was because of their fortunate constitution and social, public and free spirit.[3] He even has a backhanded plea for historical tolerance by condemning those who, for want of learning, make the present age their standard, and imagine "nothing barbarous or savage but what is contrary to the manners of their own time"

---

[1] *Hist. of Crit.*, III. 157—159.

[2] *Characteristics*, I. 141, 142, 171—2, 179—80, 249—50, and II. 257.

[3] I. 143, 154—5, and II. 241—2.

(I. 177). All this is merely stated, it is not proved except by the use of an "if" and a "naturally". Shaftesbury is not worth much to us.

Omitting Rowe for the present, Steele and Addison come next. Steele's positive value as a critic is also sometimes overrated.[1] What influence he exercised, however, was rather on the side of liberty. He gives occasional brief appreciations of Shakespeare, but quotes *Henry IV* as tragedy.[2] In *The Guardian*, 12, he protests against those who judge by narrow rules and will not be pleased except by certain systems and schemes of satisfaction (XIII, 126—27). Because he found in *Solomon's Song* that "the ideas were so exquisitely soft and tender", he paraphrased it in modern English verse (X. 23—26). In *Spectators* 366 and 406 he translates and praises two Lapland love songs.[3] But he has one passage in his essay on *Raillery and Satire* in a comparison of Horace and Juvenal where he shows something of the real historical point of view. The satirists differ because they lived in different times. Society was entirely corrupt in Juvenal's time; in Horace's time there were but petty impolitenesses and affectations to satirize. The result is seen in the lightness of Horace's style and material and the savageness of Juvenal's attacks (IV. 268—269). This covers nearly two pages in *Tatler* 242 and in comparison to the smallness of Steele's total critical output this, with the other passages cited, puts him on the way to the light.

---

[1] Wendt's *Steeles Literarische Kritik über Shakespeare* probably makes too much of Steele's influence.

[2] *British Essayists*, II. 36—38.

[3] The first translation is ascribed to Ambrose Philips, IX. 315—17; XI, 102—3.

Addison, of course, weighs much heavier in the general critical scales than Steele or Shaftesbury, though opinions differ somewhat as to his absolute value in criticism; but there is no doubt about his doing a beneficent work for his time, even if he used its standards to secure ends, which, without his help, could not so well have been reached. His larger and more important groups of essays in criticism are in general of little worth to us. His series of essays on *Wit* (Spec. 58—62), on ballads (Spec. 70, 74, 85), on Milton (Spec. 267—369) and on the *Pleasures of the Imagination* (Spec. 411—421) were of distinct worth, not only because they probably expressed Addison's real critical opinions, but also because they reached a wide audience and helped to ban false wit and to encourage appreciation for Milton and for something called imagination.

When we come to look into his methods in the examination of the ballads and of Milton, however, we find he justifies them as Harrington tried to justify Ariosto, by comparison with classic models and by the application of the rules. Addison confesses to a real love for folk songs, but to us it seems ridiculous to prove the worth of *Chevy Chase* by the rules of the epic and compare it to Homer and Virgil, and equally ridiculous to find the *Children in the Wood* compared to Horace. It seems hardly so ridiculous, however, when we remember that only in this way could he gain any hearing for his simple favorites and that is the reason he supports himself "by the practice and authority of Virgil".[1] His method with *Paradise Lost* was probably in his opinion the best, and it

[1] *Works*, II. 388.

served his purpose "to examine it by the rules of epic poetry" (III. 177). Yet his aim was consistent in all four of these larger series of essays; he was trying in a definite and connected way to improve the taste of his readers (III. 393).

In the essay on *Taste* (Spec. 409), in which Addison states his whole critical aim, we find also not only the acknowledgement of the "absolute necessity" of the rules, but a bit of sincere rebellion against the same "mechanical rules." He wants criticism to "enter into the very spirit and soul of fine writing;" besides the rules "there is still something more essential to the art, something that elevates and astonishes the fancy, and gives a greatness of mind to the reader, which few of the critics besides Longinus have considered" (III. 392). That is, the neo-classic system no longer satisfies and he wants to get at the reason in the work of art and in the mind of the reader for the pleasure produced by "a noble work." But his solution in *The Pleasure of the Imagination* does not wholly reach our case. The essay on *Genius* (Spec. 160) is another solution, offered before the problem itself was proposed. When he recognizes the two great classes of geniuses, and praises that "something nobly wild and extravagant" in those "great natural geniuses" who were formed "without any assistance of art or learning" and praises Homer, and the Old Testament still above Homer, and adds "our countryman Shakespeare" as a remarkable instance of this kind of genius, he has found one clue that will lead him out of the labyrinth of rules. In discussing the second class, those formed by rules, he realized that "an imitation of the best authors is not to compare with a good original (II. 504—506).

This is certainly good material for Young. One essay in the *Imagination* series, *The Fairy Way of Writing*, not only praises "the pleasing kind of horror" supernatural beings bring into poetry, and claims that "Shakespeare has incomparably excelled all others," but also accounts for the excellence of this "fairy way" in English poetry by the nature of the English people, their fancifulness, gloominess and melancholy (III. 422—423). This is a positive statement of the influence of national characteristics.

Addison's praise of the Bible as literature, like his dissatisfaction with the rules and his exaltation of natural genius, really contributes to the downfall of pseudo-classicism and therefore indirectly to the assumption of the historical point of view. This appreciation is scattered throughout his work. I have already cited *Spectator* 160, but praise of the beauty, the pathos, the sublimity, the exquisiteness of various parts of the Bible can be found also in Numbers 177, 333, 399, 405, 441, 453, 489, and 571. When a man praises oriental style at the expense of the occidental, praises it for its animation, warmth, ardor and intensity and then asserts that Homer and Pindar, if literally translated like the Bible, would show a comparative poverty of the imagination (III. 383) he is almost a traitor in the orthodox camp.

Hurd asserts in a footnote (V. 214) that there is no doubt of the genuineness of *A Discourse on Ancient and Modern Learning*, that Addison wrote it in his younger days (presumably while the Quarrel was raging) and later incorporated parts of it in his Milton papers.[1] Addison's

[1] Spingarn's incidental mention of this essay (he apparently accepts its authenticity) gives no indication of its value. Cf. *Seventeenth Century Essays*, I. lxxxviii.

theme in this essay is the different effects produced by a given piece or body of literature upon its contemporaries and upon readers of later ages. This is clearly a question of the practical application of the historical point of view. One special virtue of the essay is that it makes it entirely clear that it is impossible for Homer, say, to mean the same to ancient Greeks and to modern Englishmen. He thinks that his own age "takes the beauties of an ancient author, as much as 'tis possible for it at so great a distance of time;" the ancients got from the work of art certain pleasures "which we at present are not capable of" and at the same time the moderns can "discover several graces that arise entirely from the antiquity of an author" (V. 214). The distinct advantages of the contemporaries and fellow countrymen of an author are that, first, they know all the allusions to persons, poems, pictures, etc., they understand all the suggested humor and other suggestive qualities of style (pp. 214—219). Secondly, they know the scenes of the poems—"they lived, as it were, on fairy ground, and conversed in an enchanted region, where everything they looked upon appeared romantic, and gave a thousand pleasing hints to the imagination" (p. 220), and he illustrates the force of a local legend in Virgil by a comparison with the English Arthurian romances and *Guy of Warwick* (p. 220). Then they felt the force of the patriotic appeal by the choice of national heroes (p. 221). Their great orations had more effect because of phases of the art we may not know (p. 222).

Finally they got a beauty from the sound and harmony of their language which hits deaf ears with us. Here he insists that "different nations have different tastes" in the arts, music, for example: "whether or not it be that, as the temper of the climate varies, it causes an alteration in the animal spirits, and the organs of hearing; or as such passions reign most in such a country, so that the sounds are most pleasing that most affect those passions; or that the sounds, which the ear has ever been most accustomed to, insensibly conform the secret texture of it to themselves, and wear it in such passages as are best fitted for their own reception; or, in the last place, that our national prejudice makes everything appear odd to us that is new or uncommon: whether anyone or all of these reasons may be looked upon as the cause, we find by certain experience that what is tuneful in one country is harsh and ungrateful in another. And if this consideration holds in musical sounds, it does much more in those that are articulate; because there is a greater variety of syllables than of notes, and the ear is more accustomed to speech than to songs." And he ends this illuminating paragraph with, "Thus we see how time has quite worn out or decayed several beauties of our ancient authors" (p. 223).

He then proceeds to show what the old authors have gained from their great age. We have lost all the low and base effects in allusions and in that familiarity which breeds contempt (p. 224). Proper names that may have had low associations for the author's contemporaries now "have the same effect upon us as those of romance, because we meet them nowhere else but in books" (p. 225) —a highly interesting comparison! The same principle applies to names of places and plants and animals—and "Thus has time mellowed the works of antiquity" (pp. 226 to 227).

Why this important essay of Addison's is not mentioned by Saintsbury and Hamelius, I do not know. So far as I know Addison's authorship has not been disproved, and Hurd's positive opinion must fix this as a part of the Addisonian canon until it is proved to belong to someone else. Its importance as both a theoretical statement, and, to a certain degree, a practical application of the historical point of view is beyond question. Addison believed in a standard of taste, the test of which is an appreciation of the great ancients and the approved moderns (III. 387 f.). He granted the necessity of the rules and applied them, even to Shakespeare (II. 309 ff.). But he was dissatisfied with them, he exalted genius and the supernatural and the literature of the Bible, and finally in the essay on *Ancient and Modern Learning* he furnished a very good example of a "relative aesthetic" in the heyday of seventeenth and eighteenth century orthodoxy.[1]

Before taking up the Shakespeare essays Welsted's *Dissertation Concerning the Perfection of the English Language, the State of Poetry, etc.* (1724) should be discussed. Welsted's earlier *Remarks on the English Poets* in connection with his first edition of his translation of Longinus (1712) is one of the essays I have been unable to get, but Saintsbury's summary shows that being considered an enemy by Pope did not necessarily make him a bad critic. It is certainly to his credit that he published two English translations of Longinus. The *Dissertation* is not unpleasant reading, though very philosophical indeed. He has a new idea on the downfall of Rome: "The Beauty of the *Roman* Language began to fade soon after the Subversion of the Commonwealth, and was owing to it, as the Loss of their Liberty made way for that Inundation of barbarous Na-

[1] Saudé's *Grundlagen der literarischen Kritik bei Joseph Addison* is the best special study of Addison I have found.

tions" (p. XI); that is, the barbarians alone did not kill Latin literature, and they would never have come had Rome kept her liberty. "Things come by those that are past", and the past teaches us that the "Arts and Sciences, with their train of Blessings," visit in their turn all parts of the globe and leave each part sunk in desolation and barbarism, and he considered it possible that civilization might desert Europe for America sometime (p. XI—XII),—a doctrine shared at almost the same time by Du Bos. He goes further than Addison in condemning the rules. They are good only as comments on "the mighty Originals" which were produced without them and those who have followed them closest have been the worst poets. He, too, says the rules merely touch the externals, "the Secret, the Soul of good Writing is not to be come at thro' such mechanic Laws", and he proceeds to devote twenty pages to the destruction of the rules in favor of originals. One begins to see why Pope might hate Welsted, and where again Young might get some material.

## 3. The Shakespeare Essays.

Rowe's *Some Account of the Life, etc. of Mr. William Shakespear* (1709) was prefixed to the pioneer eighteenth century edition of Shakespeare. The "etc." of the title about represents its critical value. "Trage-comedy was the common mistake of that age," but because it has become so agreeable to the English taste—perhaps it will have to remain.[1] He is apologetic for Shakespeare's dramatic mixture and explains his numerous errors as the vice of the times. Since he lived under the "mere light

---

[1] *Eighteenth Century Essays on Shakespeare,* ed. by D. Nichol Smith, p. 10.

of nature and was ignorant of the written rules", it would be hard to judge him by a law he knew not of (pp. 15—16). In other words Rowe enters a plea of guilty for the prisoner at the bar, but recommends him to the mercy of the court.

Pope is so evidently a leader of the orthodox that little could be expected of him in the historical spirit. His "Discourse on Pastoral Poetry," written at sixteen, is wholly pseudo-classical.[1] In spite of a line or two like "Religion, country, genius of his age," and "Snatch a grace beyond the reach of art," the *Essay on Criticism* (1711) is the epitome of pseudo-classicism (I. 85—126). The Pope-Walsh correspondence on the *Pastorals* (1706) is of the same stripe and can be characterized by a single sentence of Walsh: "The best of the modern poets in all languages have nearest copied the Ancients" (VII. 46). The *Preface to the Iliad* (1715) is also in method and principle largely on the same side. Two comparisons of Homer to the Bible (VI. 306 to 319), and the statement that his defects come "wholly from the nature of the times he lived in", and the advice to redouble our pleasure by considering that we are "stepping almost three thousand years back into remotest antiquity"—these are the only liberal things in the *Preface* and they are very mildly liberal. In the *Preface to Shakespeare* (1725) we learn that Shakespeare is the best subject for criticism, because he furnishes the most numerous and the most conspicuous instances of both "Beauties and Faults of all sorts." Yet—"If ever any Author deserved the name of an Original it was Shakespear." He is an instrument of Nature, and he knew the world by Intuition.

---

[1] *Works,* I. 3—8.

He was a born Philosopher and Man of the World, as well as Poet—the doctrine of Dryden that Shakespeare is "naturally learned." Finally Pope writes a sentence, that, standing alone or supported by other similar principles, might lead far—"To judge therefore of *Shakespear* by *Aristotle's* rules, is like trying a man by the Laws of one Country, who acted under those of another."[1] This is Farquhar's figure but in intention only another form of Rowe's apology. Then another reason for Shakespeare's blunders in art is due to the fact that he was an actor and considered that to please his audience was the author's chief business (p. 50). Quite clearly Pope is no prophet of the new era.

The other Shakespearean critics before Johnson can be quickly disposed of. Theobald's edition (1733) deserves great credit for its exposure of Pope's blunders, but not so much for the value of the *Preface*. In the *Preface* he takes material from others and re-states it, generally, however, to improve it. He quotes Rowe to the effect that "the Knowledge of an Author may, perhaps, sometimes conduce to the better understanding of his Works".[2] Then he tries to show, what Rowe did not, the influence of the ease and sweetness of Shakespeare's temper on the facility of his writing and takes up Pope's suggestion of the evil influence of Shakespeare's profession as an actor and turns that to good, since it gave the author "an Advantage and Habit of fancying himself the very Character he meant to delineate" (p. 73). Shakespeare's blunders in his historical plays are not at all due to ignorance but to the "too powerful Blaze of his Ima-

[1] Nichol Smith, pp. 47—50.

[2] *Ibid.*, p. 65.

gination" (p. 76). Finally he takes up Temple's views as to the historical reasons why English comedy is so good[1] and adds something Temple did not furnish—the original characters in English life, "owing their immediate Birth to the peculiar Genius of each Age, an infinite Number of Things alluded to, glanced at, and expos'd must needs become obscure, as the *Characters* themselves are antiquated and disused". Therefore the critic must assume the historical point of view, "be well vers'd in the History and Manners of his Author's Age, if he aims at doing him a Service."[2] Theobald deserves the credit not only for stating the historical point of view but also for assuming it himself, so far as he was able.

Hanmer's *Preface* to his edition of Shakespeare (1744) is merely apologetic and patriotically boastful of Shakespeare's high place in the drama.[3] Warburton's *Preface* (1747) is more remarkable for its bitter attack on Theobald than for its original matter. He does say, however, that though, as Pope had said, Shakespeare furnishes the greatest field for criticism, "yet it is not such a sort of criticism as may be raised mechanically on the Rules which *Dacier*, *Rapin*, and *Bossu* have collected from Antiquity; and of which such kind of Writers as Rymer, Gildon, Dennis, [unfair to Dennis, of course], and Oldmixon, have only gathered and chewed the Husks;" and neither is it to be of the nature of *Spectator* criticism—Warburton still fights all Pope's enemies—but "by those only Laws and Principles on which he wrote, *Nature* and *Common-Sense*".[4]

---

[1] Cf. Spingarn, III. 104 ff.

[2] Nichol Smith, p. 84.

[3] *Ibid.*, pp. 94—95.

[4] *Ibid.*, p. 105.

It is to be feared that it is not so much an enemy of the rules who is speaking here, but only Pope's friend.

Three years after Warburton's *Preface* Johnson began his critical work in the *Rambler* (1750–52), and he continued to write criticism for over thirty years. It need scarcely be repeated that in the main Johnson is a pillar, the last pillar, if you will, of critical orthodoxy. This appears all through his work, from No. 3 in the *Rambler*, through the *Idler* (1758—60), *Rasselas* (1759), the Shakespeare *Preface* (1765) and on into the *Lives of the Poets* (1779—91), completed only three years before his death. He failed to respond to the new critical influences set in motion by the Wartons, Hurd and others. Yet Johnson's strong native endowment of commonsense often overcame his prejudices and his conservatism. I shall spend little time here in pointing out his orthodoxy, but it is not always extreme and sometimes disappears altogether.

One of the landmarks of Johnson's orthodoxy is his conception of the judicial, dogmatic function of criticism as found in *Ramblers* 3 and 92. In the last he grants that a standard of beauty is "different in different minds, and diversified by time and place", and in many cases it is apparent that "this quality is merely relative and comparative"; but it is the specific duty of criticism "to establish principles" and thereby explain the pleasures "which depend on known causes and rational deductions", and to leave aside those "inexplicable elegancies which appeal wholly to the fancy . . . the enchantresses of the soul".[1] That is, criticism shall control the fancy or ignore it. Another of his favorite principles, the doctrine of generalized nature, the type, not the individual, had been

[1] *British Essayists*, XVII., 181—182.

expressed as a part of the neo-classic doctrine of decorum from the time of Whetstone. Johnson clings to it throughout. It is found in *Rambler* 36[1]; and again in the famous tenth chapter of *Rasselas*, where the whole duty of the poet is prescribed and it is *not* to "number the streaks of the tulip"[2]; and this is repeated in the *Preface.*[3] The romantic conception of the superiority of individual images for poetic purposes had been expressed by Temple over half a century before Johnson's *Rambler* essay came to the support of the older doctrine.[4]

Yet there are a few compensations in Johnson. His famous attack on the rules is found in *Ramblers* 152, 156 and 158. Rules "enacted by despotic antiquity" like the unity of time and the rule for a single plot, "arbitrary edicts of legislators authorized only by themselves," and even the examples of writers of genius, are all unsafe.[5] In the *Preface* he devotes several pages to an attack on the unities and he reaches the probable conclusion that Shakespeare did know the rules and deliberately disobeyed them. The "comprehensive genius of Shakespeare" honored itself in breaking "rules merely positive", even if he "deviated from them by happy ignorance."[6] Johnson's more direct attitude on the historical point of view is shown in his complimentary letter to Thomas Warton on the publication of his *Observations* on the *Faerie Queene.* He praises Warton for indicating the only way in which the

---

[1] *Brit. Es.,* XVI. 273—278.

[2] *Select Works,* pp. 256—287.

[3] Nichol Smith, p. 114.

[4] Spingarn, *Crit. Essays,* III. 103—104.

[5] *Brit. Es.,* XVIII. 139, 147.

[6] Cf. Nichol Smith, p. 127—131.

older English authors can be studied with success.[1] When he wrote to Joseph Warton on the publication of his *Essay on Pope* he had not read "above ten pages,"[2] and it is possible he would not have been so cordial had he read more. In *Idler* 68 he shows a spirit of tolerance toward the unlettered invaders of Rome not common among neo-classicists.[3] Even in the tenth chapter of *Rasselas* he wants the poet to "divest himself of the prejudices of his age and country"[4]; but this may be a part of his theory of generalized nature. Finally as a part of his defence of Shakespeare against those who charge him with ignorance comes the statement already quoted: "Every man's performances, to be rightly estimated, must be compared with the state of the age in which he lived, and with his own particular opportunities".[5] Johnson perhaps did not mean by this exactly what we should mean, but he meant considerably more than Pope by "Religion, country, genius of his age."

The only work of Reynolds falling in our period are his essays in the *Idler* (1758—60). The foundation of his later *Discourses* appears here, and, though he did not write on Shakespeare, it is better to treat him with Johnson, where he belongs. The three essays on *False Criticisms on Painting* (*Idler* 76), on the *Grand Style of Painting* (79) and on the *True Idea of Beauty* (82) contain two principles of importance, the exaltation of "the great and general ideas which are fixed and inherent in universal nature"[6] (only Johnson's generalized nature), and an attack

---

[1] Boswell's *Life*, I. 179.
[2] *Life*, I. 62. — [3] *Brit. Es.*, XXVII. 282.
[4] *Select Works*, p. 287. — [5] Nichol Smith, p. 132.
[6] *Brit. Es.* XXVII. 318—319.

on the kind of critic "who judges by narrow rules, and those too often false, and which, though they should be true, and founded on nature, will lead him but a very little way towards a just estimation of the sublime beauties in works of genius; for whatever part of any art can be executed or criticized by rules, that part is no longer the work of genius, which implies excellence out of the reach of rules."[1] This last is going farther than Johnson, as far as anybody can well go, but the doctrine of general ideas, of the type rather than the individual is still pseudo-classical.

For convenience it will be well to mention Farmer's *Essay on the Learning of Shakespeare* (1767) here and then go back to more important men. Farmer condemns absolutely the attempts of learned critics "to trace Shakespeare in the writings of the Ancients," for "Nothing but an intimate acquaintance with the Writers of the time, who are frequently of no other value, can point out his allusions, and ascertain his Phraseology."[2] Farmer understands what is necessary to explain Shakespeare, but such learning is only a means to an end and that is the appreciation of Shakespeare.

## 4. From Blackwell to Wood.

So far in this chapter, outside of Addison's essay on the *Ancient and Modern Learning*, there has been less direct material on the historical point of view, less direct assertion of its necessity or less practical use of it, than had already appeared at the end of the sixteenth century and toward the end of the seventeenth. But if we go

---

[1] *Brit. Es.*, XXVII., 306—307.

[2] Nichol Smith, pp. 170, 214—215.

back now to Blackwell and then, excluding those already discussed, look at the other men who wrote between 1750 and 1770, we shall find contributions to the development of the historical point of view of great importance in both quantity and quality.

Blackwell's *Enquiry into the Life and Writings of Homer* (1735)[1] performed a service for criticism all the more noteworthy because it came twenty or thirty years before similar work was done by the Wartons and Hurd. It was Blackwell who expressed fully for the first time two ideas destined to be fruitful later, that Homer's greatness is to be accounted for largely as the result of a remarkable combination of circumstances and that he must be considered as a "naturall" poet.[2] In 1735 it was highly improbable that either Blackwell or any one else could conceive of the *Iliad* and the *Odyssey* as other than the work of one definite man; Vico's anticipation of the later views of Wolf and the writers of the nineteenth century was the single, but notable, exception to the rule.[3] For Blackwell, then, as for Wood later, Homer remained a distinct personality. Blackwell's great merit, however, is that he made the first extended application of the historical method to a single important literary figure. His key question, to which his whole book is an answer, is phrased as follows: "By what Fate or Disposition of things it has happened, that None have equalled him in Epic Poetry for two thousand seven hundred Years, the Time

---

[1] The *Enquiry* is not easily found, but Volkmann's excellent summary in his *Geschichte und Kritik der Wolfschen Prolegomena zu Homer* (pp. 14—20) makes the essentials of Blackwell's views accessible.

[2] Cf. Volkmann, p. 20. — [3] Cf. *supra*, p. 25.

since he wrote; Nor any, that we know, ever surpassed him before" (p. 2). Declaring that there is no miracle in the case, two pages later he states his general answer to the problem he had proposed to himself: "That Homer's Poems are of Human Composition; inspired by no other Power than this own natural Faculties, and the Chances of his Education: In a word, That a Concourse of natural Causes, conspired to produce and cultivate that mighty Genius, and gave him the noblest Field to exercise it in, that ever fell to the share of a Poet" (p. 4). Blackwell believed that even genius must be educated, though not necessarily through books or conscious study of rules. Homer is not likely to be repeated, because such an unusual combination of favoring circumstances is not likely to occur again. This combination is made up as follows: (1) Homer was one of the greatest geniuses; this genius was educated through, (2) the happiest climate, (3) the most natural customs, (4) the boldest speech, (5) the most expressive religion; and (6) it had the richest material of the world to work with for epic purposes. Because of this unique combination of forces, and not from any one alone, Homer was enabled to create the *Iliad* and the *Odyssey*.

After discussing the influence of climate, the rapid change in national life from peace to war and back again, and the resulting exaltation of patriotism, the independence and individuality of character yet unhampered by rigid conventions, the natural flexibility and poetic force of the language at that time, and the high regard paid to poets as inspired religious teachers, he proceeds to show the good luck it was for Homer to be a wandering bard, a "natural" poet, an entertainer, who was received by the highest but must entertain. All this is what enables Volkmann to say, "Homer, ein Günstling der Zeit, hat Blackwell zuerst gesagt, und Herder hat es ihm später bloß nachgesprochen".[1]

Space will not permit me to quote Blackwell at length, much as I should like to do so; yet it is only fair to give some further particulars. In his discussion of climate he cites Hippocrates and Galen as to the influence of physical forces (p. 6 f.). In his treatment of social forces he insists on the influence of "The State of the Country, where a person is born and bred; in which I include the common Manners of the Inhabitants, their Constitution civil and religious, with its Causes and Consequences" (pp. 11—12). After pointing out the difference between general social and communal forces and the individual influences of "Private Education" and "the particular way of Life", he proceeds: "From these Accidents[2], My Lord, Men in every Country may be said to draw their Character and derive their Manners. They make us *what we are*, in so far as they reach our Sentiments and give us a peculiar Turn and Appearance: A Change in any one of them makes an Alteration upon *Us*; and taken together, we must consider them as the Moulds that form us into those Habits and Dispositions, which sway our Conduct and distinguish our Actions" (p. 12). He follows this with an extensive account of the historical stage in the civilization of Greece which served as the source of Homer's ideas and of his pictures of "manners," and which also furnished him a language at exactly the right stage in its development to express such ideas and such manners.

[1] Work cited, p. 20.

[2] Cf. Rymer's use of this word, *supra*, p. 84.

This latter was made possible because the progress of speech is dependent on historical conditions, because there is "a necessary Connexion between the Dispositions of a Nation and their speech" (p. 44). Later—in 1735!—he boldly commits "something like Treason in Apollo's Court" by saying that "a *polished Language* is not fit for a great Poet" (p. 71). He asserts as the reason for clusters of great men appearing together in certain ages that "It is the *different Periods* naturally succeeding in the *Progression of Manners*, that can only account for the Succession of Wit and Literature" (p. 76). . . . "For they are settled and uniform Causes and never fail to work their Effect, unless when external Violence hinders their Operation" (p. 77). In contrast to the pseudo-classic condescension of his age toward the unlearned Shakespeare, he boldly declares: "That Homer's being born poor, and living a stroling indigent Bard, was in relation to his Poetry, the greatest Happiness that cou'd befall him" (p. 103). Because Homer's poems "were made to be *recited*, or sung to a *Company*", Blackwell "ventures to affirm, that whoever reads not *Homer* in *this View* loses a great Part of the Delight he might receive from the Poet"; for true appreciation can come only when "we put ourselves in the place of his Audience" (p. 118).

How far Blackwell could have got help from previous English criticism in explaining Homer's greatness as the peculiar effect of his environment upon his genius, the course of this study has made plain. He quotes Temple's Essay on *Poetry* with great respect (p. 71) and cites Addison's "beautiful Essay upon the Pleasures of the Imagination" (p. 148); but his praise for Pope's *Homer* and Pope's criticism is very moderate (p. 325). Yet he could have had only hints from his predecessors, English or foreign, for his particular task. That he consciously undertook such a task and succeeded so well is what made him so influential later. His book reached a third edition by 1757 and he was not only directly influential on Brown and Wood and Herder, but, through his emphasis on the "natural" character of Homer's poetry and the simplicity of life of which it was the direct result, he helped to prepare the way for the reception of *Ossian* and the Scandinavian poetry and the native English ballads.

Hume is more the philosopher and historian than the critic, but when he touches literature at all, if he considers it from his natural philosophical bent, such a tendency ought to make his ideas so much the more important for our purpose. His *Rise and Progress of the Arts and Sciences* appeared as early as 1742, and his *Standard of Taste* not until 1757. He believes it is impossible for the arts and sciences to arise without free government.[1] Then he illustrates this by the analysis of conditions in early Greece (p. 182), an analysis familiar to us in Wotton, Shaftesbury and Blackwell. But he thinks the arts can be transplanted, and that a republic is most favorable to the growth of the sciences, but "a civilized monarchy to that of the polite arts" (pp. 184—185). Since he believes that the arts can be transplanted we are not surprised when he says, "The models left us by the ancients gave birth to all the arts about 200 years ago" (p. 195). In the essay on *National Characters* (1748) he categorically denies "that men owe anything of their temper or genius to the air, food, or climate" (p. 246); and yet in the essay on

[1] *Essays*, I. 177.

*Tragedy* in 1757 he cites Du Bos as one of the few critics "who have had some tincture of philosophy" (p. 259). He attributes the similarities of national character rather to imitation, "a sympathy or contagion of manners, none of the influence of air or climate,"[1] and he attempts to prove it by running over the globe and revolving the annals of history. He follows Shaftesbury closely in his treatment of the standard of taste. The variety is obvious, but it is possible for both poet and critic to *approach a standard*, the poet through genius or observation (p. 270), the critic through "Strong sense, united to delicate sentiment, improved by practice, perfected by comparison and cleared of all prejudice" (p. 278—79). Yet he recognized fully what stands in the way of an absolute fixed standard, "the different humours of particular men," and "the particular manners and opinions of our age and country" (pp. 280—81). In insisting on freedom from prejudice on the part of the critic, he expresses fully the principle of historical tolerance, certainly a vital part of the historical point of view. If a critic is to perform his function properly, if of a different age or nation, he "must have all these circumstances in his eye, and must place himself in the same situation as the audience," that is, the original audience, "in order to form a true judgment";[2] it is no true critic, who, "full of the manners of his own age and country, rashly condemns what seemed admirable in the eyes of those for whom alone the discourse was intended" (pp. 276—277). In his definite search for the social and political causes of art and in his definite statement of the principle of historical tolerance Hume must stand high in the development of the historical point of view.

---

[1] p. 249. Cf. *Supra*, p. 29. — [2] Cf. Blackwell, *supra*, p. 124.

Hume talked largely in abstractions, however; he did not apply the methods he advocated directly to great pieces of literature, as Blackwell had done and as the Wartons were doing, even while he wrote. The first edition of Thomas Warton's *Observations on the Fairy Queen of Spenser* appeared in 1754. Warton was well equipped for his task. Besides his very wide reading in Elizabethan literature, he knew the Elizabethan critics and was evidently acquainted with the whole history of criticism to his day, including the work of all his contemporaries and immediate predecessors. He knew Du Bos, Montesquieu and Voltaire, praised Theobald as against Pope (II. 264—66), and called Hurd the most sensible and ingenious of modern critics (II. 36—37). He was a leader in a revolution, of course, but he, no more than the other revolutionaries, could be always a hero. Addison had had to compromise somewhat, and Percy did afterward. The group of men writing from 1750 on were, with the exceptions already noted, against the traditional orthodoxy of their time, but they often exhibited remains of it themselves.

Thomas Warton's subject itself was revolutionary.[1] His purpose, to give a clear and comprehensive estimate of Spenser's characteristic merits and manner, could be accomplished only by assuming the historical point of view. "For this purpose", he says, "I have considered the customs and genius of his age; I have searched his contemporary writers, and examined the books on which the peculiarities of his style, taste and composition, are confessedly founded" (II. 264). Then comes his praise of Theobald for following this method[2] and his condemnation of Pope for

[1] Cf. Phelps, work cited, Ch. IV, on the Spenserian revival before Warton. — [2] Cf. *Supra*, p. 115 f.

the sneers at Theobald's efforts. Warton is, then, perfectly conscious that he is adopting a new method of critical study; he believes, and proves by his practice, that the historical genetic method is a necessity, not for its own sake as a mere antiquarian would use it, but for adequate appreciation of any poet's individual merits.

It is not worth while to quote at length from Warton's *Observations*, epoch-making though the work is. He sketches at first the prevailing literary taste when Spenser wrote, condemns him in a reasonable way for lack of unity, but then reaches that passage which gives the first strong note of revolt: "But it is absurd to think of judging either Ariosto or Spenser by precepts which they did not attend to. We who live in the days of writing by rule, are apt to try every composition by those laws which we have been taught to think the sole criterion of excellence . . . If there be any poem, whose graces please because they are situated beyond the reach of art, and where the force and faculties of creative imagination delight, because they are unassisted and unrestrained by those of deliberate judgment, it is this" (I. 15—16). This new bombshell in the pseudo-classic camp was partly prepared for by Addison's essay on genius,[1] and is another direct preparation for Young. Warton makes large use of Spenser's relation to chivalry (I. 17—65) and quotes Sainte Palaye (I. 55), the authority Hurd used later; in his treatment of the supernatural element of the romances, he discusses "the *Sagas* or antient islandic histories."[2] He understood the weaknesses of the old romances, but knew as well their literary

[1] Cf. *supra*, p. 108; and Temple, *supra*, 89.

[2] I. 64. Cf. for Warton's interest in Norse material, Farley, work cited, *passim*.

values, and especially those that contrasted with the prevailing taste in poetry (II. 267—268). Besides the conclusion already quoted another passage states the historical point of view as clearly, and with that we may leave Thomas Warton. "In reading the works of a poet who lived in a remote age," he says, "it is necessary that we should look back upon the manners and customs which prevailed in that age," and, "place ourselves in the writer's situation and circumstances," to discover "how his turn of thinking, and manner of composing, were influenced by familiar appearances and established objects." It was thus that "Spenser, from the fashions of the times, was induced . . . to become, in short, a *Romantic* Poet" (II. 87—88).

Joseph Warton's criticism in the *Adventurer* (1752 1754) appeared before his brother published the *Observations.* The papers in the *Adventurer*[1] are not especially noteworthy. He praises the Bible as literature (51, 57), writes on Homer and Shakespeare and Milton, and harks back for one essay to the Ancient-Modern controversy (129), where he concludes that the Ancients excel the Moderns in everything except humor, and the Greeks excelled partly because of "a genial climate, that gave such a happy temperament of body as was most proper to produce fine sensations."[2] He begins his work on Pope, here, also, by pointing out his remarkable facility in borrowing (63).

Joseph Warton's *Essay on the Genius and Writings of Pope* (Vol. I., 1756; 200 pp. of II. before 1762) does not offer so much as his brother's *Observations.* The *Pope* essay serves another purpose. Thomas Warton's task was

[1] *Brit. Essayists,* XX and XXI.

[2] XXI, 240. Cf. Hume, Blackwell and others.

more constructive; Joseph's task is distinctly iconoclastic. It is only after he has lowered the pedestal on which Pope's image is placed that we can see the figures of those who did work of other kinds and in other times. But even though his work is necessarily of a negative, destructive kind, he can show what is wrong only by references to what is right.

Not so much directly on the historical point of view is found here, but there is something. In discussing Pope's *Pastorals*, he explained the naturalness and charm of the *Pastorals* of Theocritus by the fact that the poet lived in the delicious clime of Sicily, and "the poet described what he saw and felt," and had no need of the artificial (I. 3—4). On the next page he condemns Pope for trying to mix Sicilian and English images and ends with the important statement: "We can never completely relish, or adequately understand, any author, especially any Ancient, except we constantly keep in our eye his climate, his country, and his age" (I. 5). This complete statement of the historical standpoint says that it is necessary not merely to the comprehension of a work of art, but also to its relish, that is, its proper appreciation. Later he praises the Bible for "the most elevated and sublime strokes of genuine poetry," and quotes Lowth's glowing eulogy of the biblical poetry as "a pattern of just criticism" (I. 11—18). He sees the influence of Pope's circumstances upon his work (I. 105—107). He sees the connection between governments and the arts and sciences.[1] In another passage where he praises "correctness" to a certain degree, he points out its cramping influence on the French, and probably begins, in English at least, the theory that

[1] I. 182—3. Cf. Hume, *Supra*, p. 125.

in "no polished nation, after criticism has been much studied, and the rules of writing established, has any very extraordinary work ever appeared." As the reasons for this he enlarges on Temple's suggestion of the stunting power of great models and learning,[1] pointing out the antagonism that exists between rules and creative imagination, between the exaltation of reason by a scientific age and the sentiment and heart necessary to true poetry (I. 206—209). And finally he combats Johnson's and Reynolds' doctrine of generalized beauty directly and with great force[2], perhaps developing again a suggestion of Temple's.[3] On the whole Joseph Warton was a fairly consistent opponent of neo-classicism, and he saw the historical point of view was one of his greatest allies against the traditional system.

Young's *Conjectures on Original Composition* (1759) was a highly important document not only in its utterances but also in its influence. When he claims that it is an original subject and that he had read nothing on it elsewhere[4],—a statement he added in the second edition—we must not admit the claim too hurriedly. From time to time throughout this study the praise of original genius has been pointed out, even as against the rules, notably in Temple, Addison, Pope and just now in Thomas and Joseph Warton.[5] Young was certainly influential, but his work had been largely mapped out by others. Since he stuck quite closely to his text, he has little chance to express

---

[1] *Supra,* p. 88. — [2] I. 133. Cf. II. 25. — [3] *Supra,* 89.

[4] Brandl's edition, *Jahrb. d. deutsch. Shakespeare-Gesellschaft,* XXXIX. 17.

[5] Cf. *supra,* from the Elizabethans down and Brandl's *Einleitung, passim.*

the historical point of view. One chance, however, he improves. There may be reasons why genius does not appear, none why it may not exist. "An Evocation of vegetable fruits," he says, "depends on rain, air, and sun; and Evocation of the fruits of Genius no less depends on externals." Then he cites the marvellous crop in Greece and Rome, and various special forms of figurative "sunshine" afforded genius in these countries.[1] But on the whole, Young's influence on the genetic conception was only indirect.

In the same year as Young's *Conjectures* the first two volumes of Sterne's *Tristram Shandy* appeared and two years later (1761) the third volume came out with its famous onslaught in Chapter XII against the rules, and the critics with their rules, compasses and stop-watches. The only thing to compare this exquisite satire to is Butler's rather coarser satire in the same cause. Sterne would walk fifty miles on foot to kiss the hand of the man "whose generous heart would give up the reins of his imagination into his author's hands."[2] In connection with Sterne another novelist writing earlier can also be cited for freedom and in praise of genius. The first chapters of each book in Fielding's *Tom Jones* (1749) are generally critical. Fielding knows he is creating a new "Kind" of writing and therefore from time to time discusses its principles, defies the critics and posits genius as the first requisite in all writing.[3] These two novelists furnish sufficient contrast to Chapter X in *Rasselas*. Johnson was writing only an expansion of the moral tales of the

[1] Edition cited, p. 27.

[2] *Tristram Shandy*, I. 160—161.

[3] Cf. the first chapters of Bks. V, VIII, IX and XIII.

*Spectator*. Fielding and Sterne were doing something new and realized it.

Goldsmith's *Present State of Polite Learning* also appeared in 1759. It is evident that the author is not wholly original in it; yet this is one of the cases where Goldsmith did not talk like "poor Poll." Requisites for the development of the arts and sciences are permanence and freedom in the state, and favorable conditions of soil and climate.[1] In the case of Ancient *vs.* Modern Goldsmith reaches a conclusion that could have prevented the whole Quarrel had others reached it earlier, that is, that both are excellent, but are excellent in different ways, and it is absurd for the critics to compare one with the other using either as a standard (pp. 26—27). He gives definite testimony to the fact that Montesquieu's genius and success has been evil in its effects in England in attempts to reduce complex phenomena to a "line of systematic simplicity" (pp. 41, 44). When Goldsmith pronounces rhymes of an "older date than either the Greek or Latin dactyl or spondee," he proves it by "the Celtic" and cites under this "the Edda of Iceland, and the Irish carols" (pp. 61—62)—a confusion, of course, but another straw pointing out the wind toward *Ossian*. In the essay on *The Polite Learning of England and France Incapable of Comparison,* he states with considerable fulness the relativity of taste and that "the laws designed to improve our taste . . . must be adapted to the genius of every people, as much as those designed to promote morality." He even doubts whether criticism is worth while or not. There are two phases to taste, a knowledge of what gives immediate sensations of beauty, and of what gives second-

[1] *Works*, II. 17.

ary sensations of beauty through its adaptability to use as well as beauty. In the latter case taste must differ "in every climate and country," and therefore, "every country should have a national system of criticism" (p. 81). Goldsmith believes, then, in spite of some orthodoxy, in a relative aesthetic.

Hurd's *Letters on Chivalry and Romance* (1762) is another landmark in the history of English criticism. Before the publication of the *Letters* Hurd had already proved his worth as a critic by his work on Horace's *Epistle to Augustus* and his *Dissertations* on *Poetical Imitation* and on *The Provinces of the Drama* (1751), sufficiently, at least, to be called by Thomas Warton in 1754 the most sensible and ingenious of modern critics.[1] Gibbon's summary and quotations from both dissertations[2]—the originals of Hurd's early essays I have been unable to find—prove that Hurd as early as 1751 was working against orthodoxy. His whole position in regard to imitation was an attempt to free authors in the main from the charge of conscious imitation,[3] the only way, according to pseudo-classic theory, in which anybody was supposed to write well. Gibbon's account shows, also, that Hurd justifies the chorus in the ancient drama by reference to historical conditions, and that he explains the coarse humor of the classic stage by reference to their free governments and democratic equality (pp. 34—39).

It is clear from Gibbon's quotations that in his *Letters on Chivalry and Romance* eleven years later, Hurd changed his material but only developed further his historical method. In the meantime he had had the advantage of

[1] Cf. *supra*, p. 127. — [2] *Miscellaneous Works,* III. 22—58.
[3] Gibbon, p. 50.

Thomas Warton's *Observations*, of Joseph Warton's *Pope*, of Hume's *Standard of Taste* and Goldsmith's *Polite Learning*, all of them expressing phases of the historical point of view. Hurd's *Letters* make only a short essay, only a hundred and twenty pages of the so-called second edition (also 1762); were it possible, large extracts should be quoted. Part of his ground had necessarily been covered by Warton's *Observations* and Hurd owns his indebtedness to the same authorities, the old romances themselves and Saint-Palaye's *Mémoires sur l'ancienne Chevalerie*,[1] and chiefly to the latter; but the argument largely and the expression are Hurd's own and there are fewer marks of direct borrowing than we have been accustomed to see.

Hurd opens with a direct statement of the remarkableness of Gothic Chivalry and the spirit of Romance that arose out of it, and assures us that nothing in human nature is without its reasons and the explanation of things that appear fantastic can be sought successfully either in the workings of the mind itself or in historical conditions (pp. 1—2). Since chivalry itself had definite causes for its birth and development and romance sprung from chivalry, to understand the latter we must study chivalry. Then he asserts the "greatest geniuses of our own and foreign countries, such as Ariosto and Tasso . . . Spenser and Milton . . . were seduced by these barbarities . . . even charmed by Gothic Romances." Then come the revolutionary questions: "Or, may there not be something in the Gothic Romance peculiarly suited to the views of a genius, and to the ends of poetry? And may not the philosophical moderns have gone too far, in their perpetual

---

[1] *Letters*, pp. 24—25.

ridicule and contempt of it?" (pp. 3—4). To answer these two questions affirmatively is Hurd's aim. Then he accounts for the origin and characteristics of chivalry (pp. 5—23), shows that Gothic and heroic manners were similar and from similar conditions, and this accounts for the mixture of the two in Tasso and Spenser (pp. 24—44). Had Homer been familiar with Gothic manners he would have preferred them to heroic manners, because of their improved gallantry, their variety and the superior solemnity of their superstition (pp. 45—55). Spenser deliberately chose to write Gothic romance and it must be so judged, and he enters later into a defense of Spenser under Gothic rules (pp. 55—56, 60—74)—even against the attack on the poet's unity of design from Warton[1]—though he thinks Spenser tried too much to "ally two things, in nature incompatible, the Gothic, and the classic unity" (pp. 70—71). He explains how a changing public taste benefited Tasso (pp. 76—77). He sketches with lively satire the history of the subserviency of English Criticism to French influence, from Davenant and Hobbes and Rymer to Shaftesbury, who "will fight with any man who contends, not that his Lordship's mistress [the *noble antients*] is not fair, but that his own is fair also," and on to Addison (pp. 80—86). He attacks the pseudo-classic conceptions of "truth" and "Nature" in behalf of poetic or imaginative truth (pp. 92—103). The last *Letters* (XI and XII) are given over to a clear exposition of how the change in taste came about and classic models and methods wholly supplanted Gothic (pp. 104—119). He ends with the memorable phrase: "What we have gotten by this revolution, you will say,

---

[1] Cf. *supra*, p. 128.

is a great deal of good sense. What we have lost, is a world of fine fabling" (p. 120).[1]

I have already pointed out that Gibbon summarized Hurd's two dissertations. His summaries and comments appear in his *Journal* under date of 1762. Still earlier (1761) he published as his first work, and in French, his *Essay on the Study of Literature.* This has nothing for us except the significant definition: "History is the science of causes and effects."[2] In his notes on Hurd's essays, however, we find more. He agrees with Hurd as to the cause of the coarse humor in the classic drama, and then continues: "but I think the influence of government upon the manners and literature of a nation, might be the subject of a very original inquiry. I have a good many ideas myself, though, as the Abbé Trubbet calls it, 'Je n'ai pas achevé de les penser'." (III. 40). In his comment on Hurd's theory of imitation, he does not agree so fully with that critic's view. But when he considers "the shifting picture of mankind" and the "extensive and infinite range of ideas," he thinks that alone is almost sufficient "to preserve genius from imitation; since to the writers of every age and country it appears in a different shape." "It is the manners," he goes on, "the government, the religion, of that age and country," which "will

[1] The sub-title of the *Letters* in the sixth edition (1788) as "Serving to illustrate some Passages in the Third Dialogue", is borne out by a reading of this dialogue on the *Golden Age of Elizabeth* (1759). Edith J. Morley's new edition, *Letters on Chivalry and Romance with the Third Elizabethan Dialogue* (London, 1911, published since the paragraphs above were written), makes the comparison of the two easy; see p. 77 and pp. 56 ff. Brilliant as Hurd's achievement is, Miss Morley overstates when she characterizes the *Letters* as a "hitherto undreamed-of point of view" (p. 7).

[2] *Misc. Works,* VII. 116.

always make him an original" (III. 56). He then applies this principle directly to Milton, who "struck out a new species of epic poetry; but he could never have done it, had not the manners of that age, attached to religion in general, and to that tenet in particular, warmed his imagination and given it a dignity, and importance, which he could never have transfused into his poem, if he had not first felt it himself" (III. 56—57). This is certainly one of the best examples we have found of the statement of the influence of historical conditions, and its applications in a notable instance. That this genetic conception of literature still interested Gibbon, can be seen in his *Journal* (July 14—16, 1764) in his discussion of "Mallet's *Introduction* to the History of Denmark with a Translation of the Edda, the sacred book of the Celts" [*sic!*]. He sees that "A valuable work might be written, giving a philosophical picture of religions, their genius, reasonings, and influence on the manners, government, philosophy, and poetry of their respective votaries" (VI. 274).

Gibbon's temperament must receive some credit for his clear insight into the causal connection between the various phases of man's activities—political, social, religious and literary. His opinions were written before he saw Winckelmann's work, and the only influences upon him were his French contemporaries, Bolingbroke, and the new school of English critics.

The material offered by the men yet to be discussed is not so valuable, except in the case of Brown, as that found in Hume, the Wartons, Goldsmith, Hurd and Gibbon. Macpherson's *Ossian* was of very great importance, but his *Dissertations* on the *Era* and on the *Poems of Ossian*

(1762)[1] need hardly be noticed. Macpherson gives evidence, however, that the new ideas of "natural" poetry, of a more primitive, a less sophisticated type, had reached him also, for he groups Bards, Greeks and Yncas together, and praises barbarous times as the best of poetic soil.[2] Blair's *Critical Dissertation on the Poems of Ossian* (1763) is worth little more. Barbarism is favorable to poetry. Blair prepares the way for Brown, or perhaps follows him, when he discusses music and song among the barbarians. He expects similarity in poetry among different barbarous peoples, though there will have to be some diversity, "occasioned by climate and genius." The so-called oriental vein of poetry is characteristic of a stage of civilization rather than of a country (pp. 49—53). After this and a little more tolerably sensible philosophizing, he passes on to his chief task, a comparison of Ossian and Homer. Blair is following Addison's example, but the point of view is changed somewhat, for now Homer is not merely a "regular" poet, by whom the "regularity" of an audacious Modern is to be tried; Homer is used here because he is nearest to the Ossianic stage of civilization, and therefore furnishes the most fruitful comparison (69 ff.). Nevertheless the two are compared through the greater part of the essay on the basis of Aristotle's rules (72—138). Blair means well here, but he is really a conservative, and not a reformer, at heart.

Gray's importance in the romantic movement has been often enough pointed out.[3] His actual critical work is extremely meager, more's the pity. The first evidence

---

[1] Perhaps 1761; cf. Phelps, work cited, p. 149.

[2] *Ossian,* pp. 17, 19.

[3] Cf. Phelps, work cited, Ch. IX, pp. 155—170.

we have of his interest in the historical point of view is in his philosophical poem on the *Alliance of Education and Government*. It was begun in 1748, but before finishing it, he read *L'Esprit des Lois* and became discouraged with his own treatment. Later he expected to finish it and prefix to it an *Ode to M. de Montesquieu*, but the latter died in 1755 and the fragment remains as first written, though we have with it Gray's own commentary and plan. The fragment itself had but six lines on the subject directly, or rather on the influence of natural conditions on human or national character, and nothing directly as to their influence on literature.[1] Gray's own comment is but a brief expansion of the six lines, to the effect that "men receive an early tincture from the situation they are placed in, and the climate which produces them," and illustrates by the different effects upon character of life in the mountains or on the plains (I. 118). The significant thing about all this was that at thirty-two, as early as 1748, Gray was attracted toward the relation between external conditions and character, that Montesquieu's work evidently powerfully affected him, and that his mind was too acute not to carry over Montesquieu's theories into literary fields. This he must have done had there been no later influence from his own contemporaries.

His expressions in prose having any relation to criticism are scattered from place to place, chiefly in his letters. His *Metrum* (1760—61) seems to be a preliminary study toward the history of poetry he had in mind. In his *Observations on Pseudo-Rhythmus* he says he thinks the Anglo-Saxons brought rhyme with them and he seems

[1] *Works*, I. 116.

sure that the common people used it first.[1] They were not taught rhyme, then, by the medieval Latin hymn writers or anybody else. His *Remarks upon the Poems of John Lydgate* shows one brief expression of the historical standpoint, when he says it is folly to judge what appealed in art in Lydgate's time by our standards; yet he himself understood and explained why reiteration as a narrative method appealed to Lydgate's contemporaries. His letters show him to have been intimate with Thomas Warton, Hurd and other leaders in the new criticism. His interest in *Ossian*, and the Welsh bards and the Scandinavian poetry and old ballads, finds expression in his letters. As a literary force, however, his achievements in poetry were so much more important, that we shall have to rest content with that, and do without the criticism.

Dr. John Brown's work as a critic has received a surprisingly small acknowledgment. Hamelius gives Brown's work in the *Essays on the Characteristics* (1751) two pages; but he gives Brown too much credit as the first to express the historical point of view in connection with literature, and misrepresents him, when he says Brown finds no other beauty in the biblical style than truth and strength.[2] We have seen that others before Brown took the historical standpoint when they considered literature, and Brown himself praises the "unmixed poetry", that is, the imaginative appeal, of the *Psalms*, *Job*, and *Isaiah*, and points out the "tenderness and true pathos" in the story of Joseph.[3] Brown does take the historical point of view here, where he considers the relation between the growth of ancient eloquence and free governments, but

[1] Cf. I. 361—75. — [2] Work cited, pp. 162—163.

[3] *Essays on the Characteristics*, pp. 379—382.

he is only following the ideas of Wotton, Shaftesbury and others.[1] He gets the better of Hume, however, when he says that, not neglect of the art of oratory, but the "Principles of the Times and the Nature of our Constitution" account for the decrease of oratory (p. 28). Both Brown and Hume must have been surprised a few years later at the power of Pitt's oratory. One good passage in the *Essays* gives the historical causes why French and English tastes are exactly reversed in pulpit eloquence and tragedy (p. 34).

Saintsbury treats Brown briefly in the chapter on *Eighteenth Century Orthodoxy*. He considers Brown's *History of the Rise and Progress of Poetry* (1764) "amusing to read," makes fun of his figures of speech (righteously) and says "For the rest, Brown rejoices and wallows in the naturalistic generalization of his century," and "Negligible as an authority, Brown deserves to rank as a symptom" (II. 497). That is, in other language than Saintsbury's, the poor fellow attempted to take the historical point of view! In fact, Brown's *History* is the earliest work I know of which attempts to show the evolution of literary forms from a common primitive trinity of arts—music, song and dance. The method and spirit of his work are wholly scientific and historical, and it is really a remarkable prophecy of Letourneau's *L'évolution littéraire dans les diverses races humaines*[2], written over a century and a quarter later.

I must not take time to quote largely, but *The Design* and a few bits must be given. *The Design* is opened by

---

[1] *Supra, passim.*

[2] Paris 1894. Cf. such books as Gummere's *The Popular Ballad* (Boston, 1907) and *The Beginnings of Poetry* (New York, 1901).

the statement that whatever passions and principles mankind has in common can be best studied, as to their origin and progress, among savages. Because scholars have studied man only in a civilized state they have failed to solve many problems open to solution. Hence Brown proposes to show the development of poetry "through its several Periods and Progressions from the first great original Fountain of *savage Life and Manners*," and he does not mean to give more facts, but to investigate "the *Causes* that *produced* them."[1] Then he traces melody, dance and poem among savages everywhere and finds universal testimony that among savages these three arts, not yet differentiated from their original indissoluble trinity, make up "the ruling Pastime, adorn the Feasts, compose the Religion, fix the Manners, strengthen the Policy, and even form the future Paradise" (pp. 11—13). These are the circumstances common to all savage life, but he understands that "Besides these, there are many peculiar Modes, which arise from their different Climates, Situations, Opinions, Manners" (p. 13). He hits the whole pseudo-classic theory of conscious, willed development of art a hard blow when he shows that "these three Sister-Graces . . . needed no Art to joyn them: For they naturally produce each other, and are naturally conjoyned in the savage and uncultivated State" (p. 40). Then he studies at length the literary evolution of Greece; he is sometimes mistaken, of course, but in the opinion of good authorities more often right.[2] He is not mistaken when he asserts that in early periods everywhere the "several Kinds of Song . . . lay confused; and were mingled

---

[1] *Hist. of Poetry*, pp. 9—10.

[2] Cf. Letourneau, work cited, *passim*.

in the same Composition."[1] He even dares to compare the Pythian Games and early tragedy in Greece to similar conditions "among the barbarous Nations of America" (pp. 108—115). And he doubts Aristotle's authority on tragedy, not merely because the facts may be against the ancient critic, but also because it is no longer "a Point of Honour to swear to the Opinions of a Master" (p. 119).

Brown, then, is in harmony with the new spirit which welcomes information about poetic beginnings. He consistently keeps to the historical point of view, and he is the author in the middle of the eighteenth century of a remarkable anticipation of modern knowledge and theories about the beginnings of art. He carried out to its sources the line of thought suggested by Puttenham and Daniel, and he could have received little inspiration from anybody, unless possibly from Blackwell.[2]

Shenstone's importance in criticism is very little. His letters show a widely diffused literary interest and acquaintanceship. About the most important of his letters published in connection with his works is the one to Graves in 1761, giving an account of his and Percy's plans for the publication of the old ballads.[3] Dr. Hecht published just last year a new collection of letters between Shenstone and Percy,[4] of decided interest, but rather to the historian of poetry than of criticism. Percy's own criticism is chiefly valuable because of its close association

[1] Cf. for a brief statement my *Dramatic Element in the Popular Ballad.* Cincinnati, 1905, pp. 9—16.

[2] Blair's suggestions could not have helped Brown in his *Rise of Poetry and Music* of 1763.

[3] *Works*, III. 321.

[4] *Thomas Percy und William Shenstone.*

with his great work. His apologetic tone in the *Dedication* and in the *Preface* was probably the right tone to gain a hearing for his protegees. In his essay on the *Ancient Minstrels* he gives what has remained essentially the conventional English view of ballad origin. He quotes Dr. Brown twice, but we could not expect him to carry out Brown's theories to a conclusion against minstrel origin of the ballads. He quotes Hurd and Mallet and Hickes and both the Wartons and was evidently closely in touch with the new critical literature; but there is practically nothing of the historical point of view. The only exception is an attempt to show that minstrels were always of the "North Countree," because the higher civilization of the south had driven them out and they could ply their trade in comfort only in the north.[1] That is certainly little enough.

Wood's Essay on the *Original Genius and Writings of Homer* (1768) states as its purpose: "If, therefore, we would do the Poet justice, we should approach, as near as possible, to the time and place, when and where he wrote" (p. viii). Then Wood actually took his *Iliad* and his *Odyssey* and followed Homer's story on his own stage, and deliberately tried to look at all the parts of the story "in the same order, in the same light and under the same point of view in which I imagine they presented themselves to the Poet's choice" (p. 5). He shows by a contrast of external conditions why the arts should begin in Egypt and be perfected in Greece (pp. 110—111). Mythologies differ because of differing natural conditions—star-worship in the desert, and dryads in the forests (p. 113). Wood

[1] *Reliques*, I. 18.

used some of Brown's material[1], but he made an entirely new use of the historical point of view by applying it directly on the scene of the literature studied.

## 5. Summary.

Wood's essay practically concludes our study. Mrs. Montagu's *Essay on Shakespear* need not be considered, since it uses in its defence against Voltaire little more than Johnson's defiance of the rules in his *Preface*. Percy's translation of Mallet's *Introduction to the history of Denmark* under the title of *Northern Antiquities* came in 1770 and closes our list.

Eighteenth century criticism had little to offer on the historical point of view in criticism in the first fifty years, except something from Addison, a bit from Welsted, and a good deal from Blackwell. After 1750, however, and before 1770, Hume, the Wartons, Goldsmith, Hurd, Gibbon, Brown and Wood developed the genetic conception rapidly. More was done in this twenty years than had been done in the whole one hundred and eighty before. A fairly complete statement of principles had been made and a few examples of their application to particular cases had been given.

[1] Cf. p. 229.

## V. Conclusion.

The aim of the introductory chapter in this study was, first, to make clear the meaning of the historical point of view as a method in literary criticism. It was shown that this standpoint in criticism was the result of two forces especially active since the middle of the eighteenth century—the increased interest in the past, connected on the literary side with the romantic movement, and the application, through the growing influence of science, of the genetic principle to the study of all phases of man's life. The two fundamental principles underlying this last force are the belief in the historical continuity and the organic unity of national or community life. As applied to literature, then, this means a study of the causal relations of other phases of man's life, past and present, to the production of literature. The result of the application of the historical point of view, if used properly as a means to an end, is a finer appreciation of literature, due not merely to the wider knowledge of the life from which it sprang, but also to the resulting historical tolerance and a wider and wiser literary and artistic sympathy. The importance of this element of criticism and the fact that its early history in English criticism had not so far been undertaken, was the incentive to this investigation.

Before proceeding to the critical texts themselves, however, I tried to sketch the foreign critical environment of the period selected, so far as it might bear directly on my special subject, and to summarize the growth of theory and practice in history proper which accompanied and reacted upon the development of the historical point of view in literary criticism.

The use of the historical standpoint and its development before 1770 was largely occasioned by systematic and successive attempts to impose on the literature of native growth rules of foreign origin, whether purely classical, or Renaissance and seventeenth century modifications of classic rules. In the sixteenth century the chief exposition of the historical point of view was occasioned by the attempt to change the national verse forms. In the seventeenth century the battle was waged mostly around the drama, though partly also around the general question of Ancients *vs.* Moderns. In the eighteenth century critical interest continued in the questions of the late seventeenth century, but special attempts were now made to justify or excuse or explain the work of the three greatest English poets of the two preceding centuries, Milton, Shakespeare and Spenser, and to point out the insufficiency of Pope, the most prominent contemporary poet. Shakespeare in the drama, Milton and Spenser in the epic, partly at least, came into their own again as against the methods, rules and general literary ideals of which Pope was the embodiment.

The fight to preserve the national tradition involved a number of subordinate things—the question of the individuality of the language, of the rights of the imagination as against reason, of genius against rules consciously adopted, of the appreciation of simpler and more natural and unaffected literature, wherever found, as against the contemporary literature of the last hundred years of the period under study. This is why it has been necessary to notice here all these topics—the nature of the national language, reason, fancy, imagination, genius born of heaven or controlled by rules, the literature of the Bible, of the early Germanic and Celtic stock, of the native stock of folk poetry, and so on. There has always been some connection between criticism and the contemporary literature produced in different periods in England, though in general the critics ran behind the literature in the Elizabethan age, kept pace with it in the late seventeenth and early eighteenth century, and, to a certain extent, ran ahead of it in the middle of the eighteenth century.

If the extracts and summaries of the preceding three chapters have accomplished their purpose, they will have shown the reader that, by the end of the period chosen, contrary, perhaps, to a vague belief held by a good many students, there was a pretty complete development of the historical point of view in both theory and practice. Moreover, this development did not occur all at once, and did not begin with Addison's consideration of the Bible as literature or Brown's *Essays on the Characteristics*, as Hamelius asserts.[1] The blooming time of the last twenty years of the period was prepared for by the critical activities of the century that preceded.

The attacks on the national literary tradition were the occasion of most of the critical activity that involved the statement or use of the historical standpoint, but not

---

[1] Work cited, pp. 162, 166.

quite of all, and its full development toward the end of the period was chiefly caused by the two great contemporary forces, by the growing reaction against pseudo-classic literature in favor of the literature of earlier ages, and by the new scientific spirit. The critics saw, however, that the best way to appreciate and to justify the new-old literature they were beginning to love was to make use of the historical point of view in its behalf.

This is no place to review the details of the last three chapters. The reader has seen, I trust, the more prominent figures, who helped toward the development of the historical standpoint, stand out clearly. In the beginning Daniel asserted the rights of the national tradition and used brilliantly an analogical argument from history in its support. Bacon called definitely for the genetic method in literary study. Cowley, Howard, Sprat, Butler, Dennis, Congreve and Dryden all helped the movement forward at times, but Temple and Wotton helped considerably more and were directly influential on later men. At the beginning of the eighteenth century, Farquhar, Shaftesbury, Steele, Welsted, Rowe, Pope, Theobald, Warburton and Johnson contributed their mites, but Addison wrought even more than he is usually given credit for. Blackwell used the method in its practical application to the greatest figure of the ancients with distinct success. Fielding and Sterne fought against their foes, possible and actual, the "rules"-critics. Hume saw the necessity for complete historical tolerance in criticism. Young exalted genius against all external rules. The Wartons applied the method brilliantly, considering their time, one constructively in favor of an older national literary hero, and the other destructively against a contemporary hero.

Goldsmith asserted the complete independence of national standards. Hurd furnished the most illuminating justification of the earlier literature and wholly by the historical method. Gibbon saw that genius in different times and places must necessarily be different and illustrated his principle by Milton's work in a way Addison could not. Macpherson, Blair, Gray, Percy and Shenstone contributed to the new conception chiefly indirectly. Brown and Wood carried the scientific method over into literature, and the former anticipated present day opinions as to literary growth.

This is the tale. The further development of the historical point of view in criticism under the influence of romanticism and of modern science is not the function of this paper.[1] I am satisfied to have defined this phase of criticism, to have pointed out its inevitable conflict with dogmatism and its aid to a true appreciative criticism, and to have shown that it reached a fairly complete development in English criticism by 1770.

---

[1] The present study is properly only an introduction to a more extended study which I hope I shall find time to complete.

# Bibliography.[1]

Smith, G. Gregory. *Elizabethan Critical Essays.* 2 vols. Oxford, 1904.

Ascham, Roger. *The Schoolmaster.* Arber's English Reprints. Birmingham, 1870.

Spenser. Edmund. *The Shepheard's Calendar*; ed. by C. H. Herford. London, 1895.

Spingarn, J. E. *Critical Essays of the Seventeenth Century.* 3 vols. Oxford, 1908—1909.

Bacon, Francis. *The Advancement of Learning.* 2 vols. London, 1898—1901.

Flügel, Ewald. Bacon's *Historia Literaria.* (*Anglia* XXI. 259—288.)

Dryden, John. *Essays of John Dryden*; ed. by W. P. Ker. 2 vols. Oxford, 1900.

Saintsbury, George. *Loci Critici.* Boston, 1903.

*Critical Essays and Literary Fragments;* ed. by J. C. Collins. (Reprint of Arber's *An English Garner.*) New York (n. d.).

Vaughan, C. E. *English Literary Criticism.* London, 1896.

Congreve, William. *The Works of.* 2 vols. London, 1774.

*British Essayists, The.* Vols. I—XXI, XXVII. Boston, 1856—57.

Smith, D. Nichol. *Eighteenth Century Essays on Shakespeare.* Glasgow, 1903.

Dennis, John. *The Comical Gallant; or the Amours of Sir John Falstaffe.* To which is added, *A Large Account of the Taste in Poetry, and the Causes of the Degeneracy of it.* London, 1702.

Dennis, John. *The Grounds of Criticism in Poetry.* London, 1704.

[1] Arranged as follows: (1) texts in English criticism; (2) histories of criticism; (3) special studies in criticism; (4) works on the historical standpoint.

Farquhar, George. *Essay on Comedy.* 1702. In *Miscellanies.* Quoted in *The Dramatic Works of Wycherly, Congreve, Vanbrugh and Farquhar*; ed. by Leigh Hunt. London, 1866.

Shaftesbury, Anthony, Earl of. *Characteristics of Men, Manners, Opinions, Times, etc.* 2 vols. London, 1900.

Addison, Joseph. *The Works of*; ed. by Richard Hurd. 6 vols. London, 1884—1888.

Pope, Alexander. *The Works of*; ed. by Mr. Warburton. 9 vols. London, 1751.

Welsted, Leonard. *Epistles, Odes, etc. With a Translation of Longinus's Treatise on the Sublime. To which is prefix'd A Dissertation concerning the Perfection of the English Language, the State of Poetry, etc.* London, 1724.

Blackwell, Thomas. *An Enquiry into the life and Writings of Homer.* London, 1735.

Volkmann, Dr. Richard. *Geschichte und Kritik der Wolfschen Prolegomena zu Homer.* Leipzig, 1874.

Fielding, Henry. *The History of Tom Jones, a Foundling.* 2 vols. London, 1900.

Hume, David. *Essays, Moral, Political, and Literary.* 2 vols. London, 1898.

Johnson, Samuel. *Lives of the Poets.* 3 vols. Oxford, 1905.

Johnson, Samuel. *Select Works.* Oxford, 1885.

Boswell, James. *Life of Johnson.* 2 vols. London, 1904.

Warton, Thomas. *Observations on the Faery Queene of Spenser.* 2 vols. London, 1762.

Warton, Joseph. *An Essay on the Genius and Writings of Pope.* 2 vols. London 1772 and 1782.

Young, Dr. Edward. *Conjectures on Original Composition*; ed. by Alois Brandl. (In *Jahrbuch der deutschen Shakespeare Gesellschaft,* XXXIX. 1—42.)

Goldsmith, Oliver. *Works.* 4 vols. New York, 1881.

Sterne, Lawrence. *The Life and Opinions of Tristram Shandy, Gentleman. The Sentimental Journey.* 2 vols. London, 1900.

Hurd, Bishop Richard. *Letters on Chivalry and Romance.* London, 1762.

Gibbon, Edward. *Miscellaneous Works.* 7 vols. Basel, 1796.

Macpherson, James. *The Poems of Ossian. With Dissertations on the Era and Poems of Ossian; and Dr. Blair's Critical Dissertation.* Edinburgh, 1894.

Gray, Thomas. *The Works of*; ed. by Edmund Gosse. 4 vols. London, 1894.

Brown, Dr. John. *Essays on the Characteristics.* London, 1751.

Brown, Dr. John. *The History of the Rise and Progress of Poetry, through its several Species.* Newcastle, 1764.

Shenstone, William. *Works in Verse and Prose.* 3 vols. London, 1791.

Percy, Bishop Thomas. *Reliques of Ancient English Poetry.* 2 vols. Berlin, 1893.

Wood, Robert. *An Essay on the Original Genius and Writings of Homer.* Dublin, 1776.

Montagu, Mrs. Elizabeth. *An Essay on the Writings and Genius of Shakespear, Compared with the Greek and French Dramatic Poets. With Some Remarks upon the Misrepresentations of Mons. de Voltaire.* London, 1769.

Saintsbury, George. *A History of Criticism.* 3 vols. Edinburgh & London, 1900—1904.

Saintsbury, George. *Elizabethan Criticism.* Chapter 14, pp. 329—355 in *Cambridge History of English Literature,* vol. III, *Renascence and Reformation.* Cambridge, 1909.

Schelling, Felix E. *Poetic and Verse Criticism of the Reign of Elizabeth.* Philadelphia, 1891.

Spingarn, J. E. *A History of Literary Criticism in the Renaissance.* New York, 1908.

Spingarn, J. E. *The Origins of Modern Criticism.* (*Mod. Phil.* I. 477—496.)

Spingarn, J. E. *The New Criticism.* New York, 1911.

Hamelius, Paul. *Die Kritik in der Englischen Literatur des 17. und 18. Jahrhunderts.* Bruxelles, 1897.

Wylie, Laura Johnson. *Studies in the Evolution of English Criticism.* Boston, 1894.

Gayley, C. M. and Scott, F. N. *Methods and Materials of Literary Criticism.* Boston, 1899.

Bohn, Wm. E. *The Development of John Dryden's Literary Criticism* (*Pubs. Mod. Lang. Assoc.* XXII. 56—139.)

Farley, F. E. *Scandinavian Influences in the English Romantic Movement.* Boston, 1903. (Harvard Studies and Notes in Philology and Literature, IX.)

Fletcher, J. B. Areopagus and Pléiade. (*Jour. of Eng. and Germ. Phil.* II. 429—453.)

Hatch, J. C. *Der Einfluß Shaftesburys auf Herder.* (*Stud. z. vergl. lit. gesch.* I. 68—119.)

Hecht, Hans. *Thomas Percy und William Shenstone.* Straßburg, 1909.

Hofherr, Albert. *Thomas Rymers Dramatische Kritik.* I. Teil: *Die Kritik Beaumonts und Fletchers.* Diss., Freiburg, 1908.

Hoskins, John P. *Biological Analogy in Literary Criticism.* (*Mod. Phil.* VI. 407—434; VII. 61—82.)

Hoskins, John P. *The Place and Function of a Standard in a Genetic Theory of Literary Development.* (*Pubs. Mod. Lang. Assoc.* XXV. 379—402.)

Jebb, R. C. *Bentley.* New York (n. d.) *English Men of Letters Series*; ed. by John Morley.

Kabelmann, Karl. *Joseph Addison's literarische Kritik in Spectator.* Rostock, 1900.

Kind, John Louis. *Edward Young in Germany.* New York, 1906.

Manly, J. M. *Literary Forms and the New Theory of the Origin of Species.* (*Mod. Phil.* IV. 577—595.)

Maynadier, Howard. *The Areopagus of Sidney and Spenser.* (*Mod. Lang. Rev.* IV. 289—301.)

Paul, H. G. *John Dennis. His Life and Criticism.* New York, 1910.

Saudé, E. *Die Grundlagen der literarischen Kritik bei Joseph Addison.* Berliner Diss., 1906.

Sherwood, Margaret. *Dryden's Dramatic Theory and Practice.* Boston, 1898.

Smith, D. Nichol. *The Functions of Criticism.* Oxford, 1909.

Spingarn, J. E. *The Sources of Jonson's Discoveries.* (*Mod. Phil.* II. 451—460.)

Wendt, Otto. *Steeles Literarische Kritik über Shakespeare im Tatler und Spectator.* Rostock, 1901.

Weselmann, Franz. *Dryden als Kritiker.* Mülheim a. d. R., 1893.

Beers, H. A. *History of English Romanticism in Eighteenth Century.* New York, 1899.

Carlyle, Thomas. *Critical and Miscellaneous Essays.* 5 vols. New York, 1899.

Roe, F. W. *Thomas Carlyle as a Critic of Literature.* New York, 1910.

Dowden, Edward. *New Studies in Literature.* London, 1895.

Gates, Lewis E. *Studies and Appreciations.* New York, 1900.

Gates, Lewis E. *Selections from the Essays of Francis Jeffrey.* Boston, 1894.

Lounsbury, Thomas R. *Shakespeare as a Dramatic Artist.* New York, 1901.

Pater, Walter. *The Renaissance.* New York, 1906.

Phelps, W. L. *The Beginnings of the English Romantic Movement.* Boston, 1893.

Saintsbury, George. *Essays in English Literature,* 1780—1860. London, 1896.

Symonds, J. A. *Essays, Speculative and Suggestive.* London, 1907.

Wernaer, Robert M. *The New Constructive Criticism.* (*Pubs. Mod. Lang. Assoc.* XXII. 421—445.)

Winchester, C. T. *Some Principles of Literary Criticism.* New York, 1902.

De Staël-Holstein, Madame. *Oeuvres Complètes.* Paris 1871.

Herder, J. G. *Werke.* In *Deutsche Nationalliteratur.* Herausgegeben von Dr. Heinrich Meyer. Stuttgart (n. d.).

Winckelmann, J. J. *Geschichte der Kunst des Altertums.* Leipzig, 1881.

Saint-Évremond, Charles de. *Œuvres.* 5 vols. Amsterdam, 1726.

Daniels, W. M. *Saint-Évremond en Angleterre.* Versailles, 1907.

Fontenelle, M. de. *Oeuvres Diverses.* 9 vols. Paris, 1715—1717.

Lombard, A. *La Querelle des Anciens et des Modernes; l'Abbé Du Bos.* Neuchatel, 1908.

Du Bos, M. l'Abbé. *Réflexions Critiques sur la Poësie et sur la Peinture.* 3 vols. Paris, 1755.

Bernheim, Ernst. *Lehrbuch der Historischen Methode.* Leipzig, 1903.

Flint, Robert. *Vico.* Philadelphia, 1884.

Flint, Robert. *History of the Philosophy of History.* Edinburgh and London, 1893.

Einstein, Lewis. *The Italian Renaissance in England.* New York, 1902.

St. John, Henry, Viscount Bolingbroke. *Letters on the Study and Use of History.* London, 1870.

Grant, A. J. *English Historians.* London, 1906.

Stephen, Sir Leslie. *History of English Thought in the Eighteenth Century.* 2 vols. New York, 1902.

Patten, S. N. *The Development of English Thought.* New York, 1899.

Cambridge Modern History, The; ed. by A. W. Ward, G. W. Prothero and Stanley Leathes. Vols. I—XII. New York, 1902—1910.

Bosanquet, Bernard. *A History of Aesthetic.* London, 1892.

Dutoit, Eugenie. *Die Theorie des Milieu.* Bern, 1899.

ten Brink, B. *Über die Aufgabe der Literaturgeschichte.* Straßburger Rektoratsrede. Straßburg, 1890.

Falkenheim, Hugo. *Kuno Fischer und die Literarhistorische Methode.* Berlin, 1892.

Dilthey, Wilhelm. *Die Einbildungskraft des Dichters.* (In *Philosophische Aufsätze.*) Leipzig, 1887.

Brunetière, Ferdinand. *Manual of the History of French Literature.* New York, 1898.

Taine, H. A. *History of English Literature.* 4 vols. Edinburgh, 1873.

Sainte-Beuve, G. A. *Nouveaux Lundis.* Vol. VIII. Paris, 1885.

Scherer, Edmond. *Essays on English Literature.* New York, 1891.

Brandes, G. *Die Hauptströmungen der Literatur des 19. Jahrhunderts.* Leipzig, 1894.

---

# Index.